DISCARD

The Boston
Massacre

FAMOUS

TRIALS

Titles in the Famous Trials series include:

The Boston Massacre

by Bonnie L. Lukes

FAMOUS TRIALS

Lucent Books, San Diego, CA

Library of Congress Cataloging-in-Publication Data

Lukes, Bonnie L.
  The Boston massacre / by Bonnie L. Lukes.
    p. cm. — (Famous trials)
  Includes bibliographical references (p.   ) and index.
  Summary: Historical examination of the aftermath, including the trials, of the Boston Massacre of 1770.
  ISBN 1-56006-467-6 (alk. paper)
  1. Boston Massacre, 1770—Juvenile literature. [1. Boston Massacre, 1770.] I. Title. II. Series: Famous trials series.
E215.4.L93 1998
973.3'113—dc21   97-27445
                                                                          CIP
                                                                          AC

Copyright © 1998 by Lucent Books, Inc.
P.O. Box 289011
San Diego, CA 92198-9011
Printed in the U.S.A.

Table of Contents

Foreword

"The law is not an end in and of itself, nor does it provide ends. It is preeminently a means to serve what we think is right."

William J. Brennan Jr.

THE CONCEPT OF JUSTICE AND THE RULE OF LAW are hallmarks of Western civilization, manifested perhaps most visibly in widely famous and dramatic court trials. These trials include such important and memorable personages as the ancient Greek philosopher Socrates, who was accused and convicted of corrupting the minds of his society's youth in 399 B.C.; the French maiden and military leader Joan of Arc, accused and convicted of heresy against the church in 1431; to former football star O.J. Simpson, acquitted of double murder in 1995. These and other well-known and controversial trials constitute the most public, and therefore most familiar, demonstrations of a Western legal tradition that dates back through the ages. Although no one is certain when the first law code appeared or when the first formal court trials were held, Babylonian ruler Hammurabi introduced the first known law code in about 1760 B.C. It remains unclear how this code was administered, and no records of specific trials have survived. What is clear, however, is that humans have always sought to govern behavior and define actions in terms of law.

Almost all societies have made laws and prosecuted people for going against those laws, but the question of which behaviors to sanction and which to censure has always been controversial and remains in flux. Some, such as Roman orator and legislator Cicero, argue that laws are simply applications of universal standards. Cicero believed that humanity would agree on what constituted illegal behavior and that human laws were a mere extension of natural laws. "True law is right reason in agreement with nature," he wrote,

7

world-wide in scope, unchanging, everlasting. . . . We may not oppose or alter that law, we cannot abolish it, we cannot be freed from its obligations by any legislature. . . . This [natural] law does not differ for Rome and for Athens, for the present and for the future. . . . It is and will be valid for all nations and all times.

Cicero's rather optimistic view has been contradicted throughout history, however. For every law made to preserve harmony and set universal standards of behavior, another has been born of fear, prejudice, greed, desire for power, and a host of other motives. History is replete with individuals defying and fighting to change such laws—and even to topple governments that dictate such laws. Abolitionists fought against slavery, civil rights leaders fought for equal rights, millions throughout the world have fought for independence—these constitute a minimum of reasons for which people have sought to overturn laws that they believed to be wrong or unjust. In opposition to Cicero, then, many others, such as eighteenth-century English poet and philosopher William Godwin, believe humans must be constantly vigilant against bad laws. As Godwin said in 1793:

Laws we sometimes call the wisdom of our ancestors. But this is a strange imposition. It was as frequently the dictate of their passion, of timidity, jealousy, a monopolizing spirit, and a lust of power that knew no bounds. Are we not obliged perpetually to renew and remodel this misnamed wisdom of our ancestors? To correct it by a detection of their ignorance, and a censure of their intolerance?

Lucent Books' *Famous Trials* series showcases trials that exemplify both society's praiseworthy condemnation of universally unacceptable behavior, and its misguided persecution of individuals based on fear and ignorance, as well as trials that leave open the question of whether justice has been done. Each volume begins by setting the scene and providing a historical context to show how society's mores influence the trial process and the verdict. Each book goes on to present a detailed and lively account of the trial, including liberal use of primary source material such as direct testimony, lawyers' summations, and contemporary and modern commentary. In addition, sidebars throughout the text create a broader context by presenting illuminating details about important points of law, information on key personalities, and important distinctions related to civil, federal, and criminal procedures. Thus, all of the primary and secondary source material included in both the text and the sidebars demonstrates to readers the sources and methods historians use to derive information and conclusions about such events.

Lastly, each *Famous Trials* volume includes one or more of the following comprehensive tools that motivate readers to pursue further reading and research. A timeline allows readers to see the scope of the trial at a glance, annotated bibliographies provide both sources for further research and a thorough list of works consulted, a glossary helps students with unfamiliar words and concepts, and a comprehensive index permits quick scanning of the book as a whole.

The insight of Oliver Wendell Holmes Jr., distinguished Supreme Court justice, exemplifies the theme of the *Famous Trials* series. Taken from *The Common Law*, published in 1881, Holmes remarked: "The life of the law has not been logic, it has been experience." That "experience" consists mainly in how laws are applied in society and challenged in the courts, a process resulting in differing outcomes from one generation to the next. Thus, the *Famous Trials* series encourages readers to examine trials within a broader historical and social context.

Introduction

In Search of Justice

O N THE NIGHT OF MARCH 5, 1770, British soldiers fired into
a jeering Boston crowd. Three men were killed instantly, a
fourth lay dying, and a fifth would die two days later. Three of
the slain were only seventeen years old.

Boston was stunned by the killings. And yet to many of the
townspeople, the confrontation came as no surprise. The stage
had been set for violence since October 1, 1768, when the soldiers first marched into Boston. Bostonians, with their intense
fear of standing armies, had hated the soldiers from the beginning. And, in turn, the young soldiers, who were daily harassed
and taunted with insults, hated the townspeople. The tension
had continued to escalate until that cold, moonlit night in March
when the British soldiers reacted with violence.

Watching the snow on King Street turn red with the blood of
their own, horrified Boston citizens vowed vengeance. Many
were tempted to take the law into their own hands. How could
there be a trial anyway? Who in the town would consent to
defend these "licentious and blood-thirsty Soldiery"?

Surprisingly, John Adams, a young patriot lawyer who
resented the soldiers as much as anyone, agreed to represent
them. "Counsel," Adams said, "ought to be the very last thing
that an accused Person should want [lack] in a free Country."

At the outset, however, the likelihood of the soldiers receiving a fair hearing did not look promising. Colonial propagandists
worked overtime producing pamphlets and cartoons that
depicted the soldiers as "bloody butchers." Silversmith and

A broadside incites fellow Americans to protest the shooting of innocent civilians by British soldiers.

patriot Paul Revere etched an engraving of the "massacre" that showed the soldiers cold-bloodedly shooting into a Boston crowd without provocation or cause. A dramatic public funeral held for the slain men added to the emotional turmoil. Twenty thousand tight-lipped spectators from Boston and its surrounding communities lined the streets to watch the funeral procession. All of Boston believed the soldiers would be convicted.

However, much more was at stake than the fate of eight frightened soldiers and their captain. The city of Boston—which had led colonial protests against Britain's attempts to tax the colonists—was considered by England to be the cesspool of colonial America. The trial would provide an opportunity to show both friends and enemies in England that Boston was not the bloodthirsty, lawless city they thought.

Moreover, all of colonial America was aware of the threat

AMERICANS!
BEAR IN REMEMBRANCE
The HORRID MASSACRE
Perpetrated in King-ftreet, BOSTON,
New-England.
On the Evening of March the Fifth, 1770.
When FIVE of your fellow countrymen,
GRAY, MAVERICK, CALDWELL, ATTUCKS,
and CARR.
Lay wallowing in their Gore!
Being *bafely*, and moft *inhumanly*
MURDERED!
And SIX others badly WOUNDED!
By a Party of the XXIXth Regiment,
Under the command of Capt. Tho. Prefton.
REMEMBER!
That Two of the MURDERERS
Were convicted of MANSLAUGHTER!
By a Jury, of whom I fhall fay
NOTHING,
Branded in the hand!
And *difmiffed*,
The others were ACQUITTED,
And their Captain PENSIONED!
Alfo,
BEAR IN REMEMBRANCE
That on the 22d Day of February, 1770
The infamous
EBENEZER RICHARDSON, Informer,
And tool to Minifterial hirelings,
Moft *barbaroufly*
MURDERED
CHRISTOPHER SEIDER,
An innocent youth!
Of which crime he was found guilty
By his Country
On Friday April 20th, 1770;
But remained *Unfentenced*
On Saturday the 22d Day of February, 1772.
When the GRAND INQUEST
For Suffolk county,
Were informed, at requeft,
By the Judges of the Superior Court,
That EBENEZER RICHARDSON's *Cafe*
Then lay before his MAJESTY.
Therefore faid *Richardfon*
This day, MARCH FIFTH! 1772,
Remains UNHANGED!!!
Let THESE things be told to Pofterity!
And handed down
From Generation to Generation,
'Till Time fhall be no more!
Forever may AMERICA be preferved,
From weak and wicked monarchs,
Tyrannical Minifters,
Abandoned Governors,
Their Underlings and Hirelings!
And may the
Machinations of artful, *defigning* wretches,
Who would ENSLAVE THIS People,
Come to an end,
Let their NAMES and MEMORIES
Be buried in eternal oblivion,
And the PRESS,
For a SCOURGE to Tyrannical Rulers,
Remain FREE.

of mob justice hovering over Boston. The other colonies would be watching closely to see which would win, the law or mob violence. For despite rebellion against laws such as the Stamp Act, which the colonists considered unjust, colonial Americans had a profound respect for the law. Boston patriots continually cited legal and constitutional grounds in their protests to England. Could they now put aside personal prejudice and uphold the law?

Finding the answer was, in John Adams's words, "as important a Cause as ever was tryed in any Court or Country of the World."

Chapter 1

Boston: City on the Brink

WHEN BRITISH SOLDIERS FIRED into a Boston crowd on March 5, 1770, it was not an isolated, unprovoked act. The presence of a standing army may have provided the catalyst, but events that led to the tragedy of that night had begun long before. Since 1765 Boston had been in a state of discontent that bordered on rebellion.

In 1765, Boston had a population of over twenty thousand people. It was the second largest city in the colonies and was dominated by two political factions, the Loyalists, otherwise known as Tories, and the patriots, or radicals. The Loyalists, as the name suggests, were loyal to the British government and supported its policies. The patriots, too, pledged loyalty to England, but they were also fiercely protective of colonial rights and often disagreed with parliamentary decisions.

Because the colonies were still associated with England, colonial Americans were ruled by the king and were expected to obey laws passed by Parliament. But by 1765, colonial assemblies had grown increasingly independent. Although government structure varied somewhat from colony to colony, all thirteen colonies had a government in which the people elected their own representatives to colonial assemblies. This direct representation differed from government in the mother country, England, where the people, whether or not they were allowed to vote, were considered indirectly represented in Parliament.

When Parliament proposed the Stamp Act in 1765, these ideological differences clashed.

The Stamp Act

Patriot John Adams, a young Boston lawyer, called the Stamp Act "that enormous engine, fabricated by the British Parliament, for battering down all the rights and liberties of America." The act required colonists to pay a tax on legal documents and other paper items. Colonial Americans called this "taxation without representation" because they had no elected representatives in Parliament. The colonies protested the Stamp Act in the only lawful way open to them: They petitioned the administration. But neither the king nor Parliament would consider their appeals.

The British Parliament required stamps such as these on all colonial publications and legal documents under the Stamp Act.

In May 1765, Boston learned that, despite colonial protests, the Stamp Act would become law in November. Surprisingly, the Massachusetts Assembly's only response was to submit a meek protest to Parliament. But then the radical *Boston Gazette* printed the just-passed Virginia Resolves. The resolves stated, in effect, that Parliament had no authority to tax the colonists. Boston, bolstered by Virginia's bold stance, emerged from its lethargy.

The Loyal Nine

Petitions, pleas, speeches, and political treatises had failed, but there was another way to protest. In Boston, a group called the Loyal Nine—soon to be called the Sons of Liberty—took the fight to the streets. The Loyal Nine included several artisans and shopkeepers, as well as the publisher of the *Boston Gazette*. None of the Loyal Nine was a member of the legislature, but they often influenced its actions. Author Dirk Hoerder describes the Loyal Nine in his book *Crowd Action in Revolutionary Massachusetts:*

> The Loyal Nine became a kind of clearing house between top leadership and crowd. Their strength was the organizational talent with which they arranged crowd action or responded to it. The informality of their connections gave them large discretionary powers.

Captain-General of the Liberty Tree

To take their protests to the streets, the Loyal Nine recruited the experts—the North and South End gangs of Boston. For years these two gangs had celebrated "Pope's Day" (Guy Fawkes Day in England) on November 5 by engaging in bloody battles with each other.

At a meeting of the Sons of Liberty, members look on as one man makes a dramatic point. The group often organized citizens to take mass action against British rule.

POPE'S DAY

Pope's Day was celebrated yearly throughout New England. It commemorated the Gunpowder Plot of 1605, when a band of Catholics in England tried to kill King James and the members of Parliament. Over the years, its anniversary had become an excuse for a celebration. An eighteenth-century almanac noted under the fifth of November: "Powder plot is not forgot. 'Twill be observed by many a sot."

In the smaller towns, the celebration resembled today's Mardi Gras and was relatively peaceful. But in Boston, where the observance was taken over by the North and South End gangs, the celebration had become a violent one.

In preparation, each gang built a huge wagon, twenty to forty feet in length and five to six feet wide. Atop the wagon, they seated a life-size figure that represented the Pope. Behind him sat a figure of the Devil, complete with horns, tail, and a pitchfork. A paper lantern illuminated the wagon. The lantern could hold as many as six people plus the lights.

The wagons paraded through the town until they met. The rival gangs then battled ferociously, each seeking to gain possession of the other's "Pope." The bloody encounters left both gang members and innocent people severely injured. In the 1764 celebration, a child fell and was killed instantly when his head was crushed by a wagon's heavy wheels.

For twenty-four hours every year, the gangs ruled in Boston; it was impossible for the town's eight to ten constables to control them. Sam Adams and the Loyal Nine sought to turn this Pope's Day violence in another direction.

The Loyal Nine, with the help of radicals like Sam Adams (John Adams's cousin), convinced the two gangs to band together and fight the tyranny of England instead of each other. Ebenezer MacIntosh, the leader of the South Enders, emerged as the leader of the united gangs. On the next Pope's Day, there would be no battles. Instead, "General" MacIntosh, resplendent in a militia uniform of gold and blue and a hat laced with gold, would march his "troops" through the streets of Boston to demonstrate unity against the hated stamps.

MacIntosh was a shoemaker who had fought in the French and Indian War. He had also fought poverty all of his life.

Because of this, it was probably easy for him to make peace with the rival North Enders, knowing that his new enemy would be people like Andrew Oliver.

The Stamp Act Riots

Andrew Oliver was the brother-in-law of Thomas Hutchinson, the lieutenant governor of Boston. Oliver was an aristocrat and a wealthy merchant; he and others like him would profit from the stamp tax. The Crown appointed Oliver to become the stamp distributor in Boston.

A detail from Paul Revere's engraving entitled "View of Year 1765," shows Andrew Oliver's effigy hanging from the Liberty Tree.

On the morning of August 14, 1765—less than three months before the Stamp Act would become law—Bostonians awoke to find an effigy of Andrew Oliver hanging from the Liberty Tree. Attached to the figure was a two-line verse: "What greater joy did New England see/ Than a stampman hanging on a tree." The effigy remained on the tree throughout the day because Governor Bernard and his council felt that "an attempt to remove it would bring on a riot."

As soon as night fell, MacIntosh and his mob removed the effigy and marched to Andrew Oliver's private dock on Kilby Street. The mob suspected that the newly erected building there was to serve as the "Stamp Office." They destroyed it in about five minutes. Then, still carrying the effigy of Oliver, they climbed nearby Fort Hill, which over-looked Oliver's house.

On the hilltop, the effigy—after being "stamped" with the feet of the mob—was burned. They then stormed Oliver's house, broke down its locked doors, and threatened to kill him. However, Oliver had long since fled to Castle William, a fortress on an island in the harbor about three miles from the town. Mac-Intosh's men contented themselves with smashing furniture and dismantling the house.

The next day, a small group of Boston's more prominent cit-izens called on Andrew Oliver and urged him to resign his com-mission as distributor of stamps. Oliver's official confirmation for the position had not yet arrived from England, but he promised to resign as soon as it did. To ensure that Oliver remembered his promise, the mob gathered that night for a bonfire on Fort Hill.

Riots Continue

For eleven days, the mob was relatively quiet. Then, on the evening of August 26, they went after the proud and haughty lieutenant governor. Thomas Hutchinson was a primary target because he was believed to support the Stamp Act. But he had also incurred the wrath of the people as a result of, what John Adams called, his "very ambitious and avaricious Disposition."

Hutchinson had "grasped four of the most important [political] offices in the Province into his own Hands." He had also secured political appointments for family members. "How tempting," his-torian Robert Middlekauff writes in *The Glorious Cause,* "to intro-duce [Hutchinson] to humility while defending colonial rights."

When the riotous mob descended on his home, Hutchinson escaped through the backyards and gardens of his neighbors. The mob then worked through the night, methodically destroy-ing the house and its contents. Only the coming of the morning light prevented them from leveling the house to its foundation.

Reining in the Mob

The mob undoubtedly went further than the Loyal Nine intended when it destroyed Hutchinson's home. And in the future, Boston's

MOB'S DESTRUCTION OF HUTCHINSON'S HOUSE

In a letter to the colonial agent in London, Lieutenant Governor Thomas Hutchinson described the ravaging of his home.

The home of Thomas Hutchinson was destroyed by angry mobs.

In the evening, whilst I was at supper and my children round me, somebody ran in and said the mob was coming. I directed my children to [dash] to a secure place, and shut up my house . . . intending not to [leave] it; but my eldest daughter . . . protested she would not [leave] the house unless I did. I couldn't stand against this, and withdrew with her to a neighboring house, where I had been but a few minutes, before the hellish crew fell upon my house with the rage of devils, and in a moment with axes split down the doors and entered. . . . Not contented with tearing off all the wainscot and hangings, and splitting the doors to pieces, they beat down the partition walls, . . . cut down the cupola . . . and . . . began to take the slate and boards from the roof. . . . The garden-house was laid flat, and all my trees, etc., broke down to the ground.

Such ruin was never seen in America. Besides my . . . family pictures, household furniture of every kind, my own, my children's and servants' apparel, they carried off about 900 pounds sterling in money, and emptied the house of everything whatsoever . . . not leaving a single book or paper in it, and . . . scattered or destroyed all the manuscripts and other papers I had been collecting for thirty years.

Sons of Liberty would maintain firmer control over "General" MacIntosh and his "troops." Nevertheless, the mob had accomplished its designated purpose. Middlekauff writes:

The opposition to the Stamp Act had expressed itself rather forcibly, no further violence seemed necessary at the end of August. The mob may have gone too far, and the town said it was sorry, but no one apologized for the riot of August 14 against Oliver, and no one repudiated opposition to taxation without consent. The riot of August 26 [against Hutchinson] may have proceeded farther than the Loyal Nine intended, but they could not have felt much displeasure that it had. Hutchinson was an enemy . . . and he had been put in his place. In only a limited sense, then, had the action . . . been too extreme.

Parliament Repeals the Stamp Act

Mob violence was not the only way colonists protested the Stamp Act. Across the colonies, merchants organized and agreed not to import British goods. Moreover, colonial intellectual leaders from nine of the thirteen colonies met in New York for the first intercolonial assembly ever held. They petitioned the king and Parliament to repeal the Stamp Act. And they drafted a joint statement resolving that "no taxes [could] be constitutionally imposed on them, [except] by their respective legislatures."

On March 17, 1766, Parliament repealed the Stamp Act. Communication was slow in the eighteenth century, and news of the repeal did not arrive in Massachusetts until May. When it did, Boston celebrated with bonfires and booming cannons. The tension that had dominated the town for over a year drained away, and Bostonians drew a collective sigh of relief. Unfortunately, the reprieve would be short-lived.

More Taxes

Soon after the Stamp Act was repealed, Charles Townshend, the acting prime minister, introduced a bill that called for new customs duties on imports from England. What alarmed the colonists about the new tax was that Townshend planned to use the revenue to pay the salaries of royal officials in the colonies, thereby making them independent of colonial assemblies.

Sam Adams and another active patriot, James Otis, sent a letter to all colonial assemblies calling for a nonimportation agreement. In the meantime, Townshend dispatched five commissioners of customs to Boston to oversee collection of the new taxes.

SAM ADAMS, FREEDOM FIGHTER

Sam Adams would be elected to the Massachusetts legislature, become a delegate to the First Continental Congress, and sign the Declaration of Independence. But in 1765, at age forty-three, he had failed at everything he tried. Then King George III and the British Parliament helped him discover his true calling.

Samuel Adams's speeches and writings helped spark the American Revolution.

Sam Adams's talent lay in political organizing. He was not an orator; he had a quavering voice, and his hands shook from palsy. Nonetheless, he could talk his way into or out of anything, and could convince anyone to follow him. He recruited members of the Sons of Liberty from the waterfront crowd as well as from Harvard graduates. By the time England passed the Stamp Act, Adams had built a strong political base.

Though he was always a rabid supporter of human rights and liberties, Adams's methods were controversial. Like his contemporaries, modern historians have been unable to determine the extent of Adams's behind-the-scenes involvement in the political unrest in Boston. He undoubtedly choreographed much of the mob violence against the merchants who refused to stop importing goods from England. He has even been suspected of initiating the harassment of the British soldiers that led to what Sam Adams himself labeled the "Boston Massacre."

No one was neutral about Sam Adams. His friends loved and fiercely defended him. His enemies hated and vilified him. One foe said that if he "wished to draw a picture of the Devil . . . he would get *Sam Adams* to sit for him."

The British Are Coming

In the summer of 1768, the political climate in Boston grew hotter. The customs officers had arrived the previous November. They had authority to enter homes and businesses on any pretense to search for smuggled goods. Bostonians despised the corrupt tax collectors and gave them as little cooperation as possible.

Angry Bostonians confine a British customs employee on John Hancock's sloop, Liberty, *in an effort to prevent him from collecting taxes.*

In June, the customs officials angered the patriots beyond toleration when they harassed John Hancock. Hancock was a popular behind-the-scenes supporter of the Sons of Liberty. When customs officials seized Hancock's sloop, *Liberty,* on a false charge of having smuggled goods aboard the boat, they were mobbed by an angry Boston crowd and forced to take refuge at Castle William.

Angry British officials immediately dispatched four regiments of troops to Boston—two from Nova Scotia and two from England. Their purpose was to bring Boston into submission as an example to the other colonies. Boston patriots recoiled at the thought of troops occupying their town. Andrew Eliot, a patriot minister, wrote to a friend: "To have a standing army! Good God! What can be worse to a people who have tasted the sweets of liberty!"

Some radicals advocated using force against the troops. But in the end, Boston offered no resistance, and in late September

1768, the two regiments from Nova Scotia sailed into Boston Harbor. The warships lined up with guns pointed menacingly at the town. On October 1, as the resentful townspeople watched, the soldiers of the Twenty-ninth and Fourteenth regiments marched up King Street with "Drums beating, Fifes playing and Colours flying." With the exception of the town Loyalists who were relieved to see the troops, the townspeople vowed to make life for the soldiers as uncomfortable as possible.

No Rooms to Let

Lieutenant Colonel William Dalrymple, the officer in command, asked the town council to arrange housing for the soldiers. The council refused on the grounds that the town was not required to provide quarters until all regular barracks were filled. They pointed out that Castle William had plenty of barrack space available. But royal officials wanted the soldiers in the town itself, not isolated out in the harbor.

Consequently, Colonel Dalrymple was temporarily forced to quarter his troops wherever he could—in tents on the common, in Faneuil Hall, and even in the Town House where the House of Representatives met. Finally, on October 27, the regiments moved

An engraving by Paul Revere depicts British troops landing in Boston in 1768. The town refused to house the troops the ships carried.

into leased warehouses. Two companies from the Twenty-ninth occupied the sugar warehouse on Brattle Street, which they named Murray's Barracks after its owner. The remainder of the Twenty-ninth, along with the Fourteenth Regiment, occupied warehouses on Griffin's Wharf and Wheelwright's Wharf.

Boston Sees Red

As expected, there was immediate friction between the soldiers and the townspeople. And it didn't help matters when the Sixty-fourth and Sixty-fifth regiments arrived from England in mid-November. Soldiers and civilians regularly exchanged verbal insults. Fistfights and brawls in taverns became a nightly occurrence.

The soldiers were limited in how far they could go in retaliating to harassment. A quick shove by a soldier could, and often did, send a civilian flying off a footbridge, but the soldiers had strict orders never to fire upon citizens. Nor were they to attack them in any other way, except on the order of an officer—regardless of the provocation. But officers themselves were hampered. They could not call out troops against citizens without a written order from a civil authority, and such an order was almost impossible to obtain.

Boston Gets a New Governor

Prior to the arrival of the troops, Francis Bernard, the royal governor, had requested leave from his duties to visit England. He received permission in the summer of 1769. Thomas Hutchinson, whose house had been sacked in the Stamp Act riots, became acting governor.

English officials had concluded by this time that the troops in Boston were serving no useful purpose.

Thomas Hutchinson became acting governor of Boston in 1769.

HIS MAJESTY'S ARMY

The mere sight of British troops on their streets and in their stores angered Boston citizens. Adults treated the soldiers with contempt. Children followed after them in the streets and ridiculed their red uniforms with taunts of "lobster-backs" and "bloody-backs." A major source of friction was that the underpaid soldiers often took second jobs for low pay. Boston's working class resented this additional competition for jobs.

Nevertheless, the townspeople sometimes pitied the young soldiers because of the harsh discipline imposed by their commanding officers. Even a minor offense like swearing resulted in a brutal beating. In the first two weeks that the troops occupied Boston, seventy soldiers deserted and hid out in the countryside. In an attempt to halt desertions, a deserter named Ames was court-martialed and sentenced to death. He was executed by a firing squad on the Boston Common. This cruel exhibition only added to Boston's distrust and fear of the occupying army.

To catch deserters, Colonel Dalrymple posted guards at the principal access roads in and out of Boston. These sentries also challenged Boston citizens leaving or entering the town—a duty they sometimes performed so zealously that the townspeople complained of physical harassment. Just as often though, a citizen would refuse to answer a sentry's challenge, then would declare the soldier had used force and bring him into court on charges of disturbing the peace. The soldiers were almost always found guilty and ordered to pay heavy fines. Soldiers with valid complaints against Boston citizens were advised by their commanding officers not to take their cases to court, because "no [justice] could be obtained for A Soldier in Boston."

Consequently, when Governor Bernard sailed for England on August 1, the Sixty-fourth and Sixty-fifth regiments accompanied him. Boston held a wild celebration. The people assumed that the other two regiments would soon follow. When they did not, hostility toward the remaining soldiers intensified.

Tension increased daily, and the strain began to take its toll. Confrontations became more frequent. To protect themselves, soldiers had to walk in groups from their barracks to their duty posts. Fights between the soldiers and the waterfront toughs not only increased in number, but they became more violent. British soldiers stormed the Boston jail and rescued a fellow soldier. Patriot James Otis was attacked by a customs agent and left with a one-and-a-half-inch gash that penetrated down to the bone of his forehead.

To add to the inflammatory circumstances, the nonimportation agreement in effect among Boston merchants since the Townshend Acts were passed would officially end on December 31, 1770. Patriots wanted the agreement extended until Parliament agreed to repeal the Townshend Acts. But the Loyalists tried to prevent its extension. Eight Loyalist merchants refused to sign a new agreement and resumed selling goods imported from England.

Picketing the Merchants

Sons of Liberty picketed the stores of these "uncooperative" merchants. Signs were placed in front of their shops, targeting them as importers. Their shops and houses were smeared with mud and feces. Broadsides (flyers), like this one posted in January 1770, were common:

WILLIAM JACKSON,
an IMPORTER; at the
BRAZEN HEAD,
North Side of the TOWN-HOUSE,
and opposite the TOWN-PUMP, in
Corn-hill, BOSTON.
It is desired that the Sons and Daughters of LIBERTY,
would not buy any one thing of him for in so doing
they will bring Disgrace upon *themselves*, and
their *Posterity*, for *ever* and *ever*, AMEN.

Theophilus Lillie was one of the merchants who refused to sign a new nonimportation agreement. On the morning of February 22, a crowd composed mostly of schoolboys—probably encouraged by the Sons of Liberty—placed an "importer" sign in front of Lillie's shop. A few minutes later, Lillie's neighbor Ebenezer Richardson arrived on the scene.

Richardson was an informer, despised by the Sons of Liberty because he had cooperated with the hated customs commissioners. The patriots considered him "the most abandoned wretch in

---

WILLIAM JACKSON,

an *IMPORTER*; at the

BRAZEN HEAD,

North Side of the TOWN-HOUSE,

and *Oppofite the Town-Pump, in*

Corn-hill, BOSTON.

It is defired that the SONS and DAUGHTERS of *LIBERTY,* would not buy any one thing of him, for in fo doing they will bring Difgrace upon *themfelves,* and their *Pofterity,* for *ever* and *ever,* AMEN.

A typical handbill used to target the shop of a Loyalist merchant who resumed selling goods from England.

America." Richardson attempted to tear down the sign, but the mob stopped him, pelting him with mud clods and stones. He was forced to retreat to his nearby home. The crowd followed.

Murder in the Street

The throng yelled curses at Richardson demanding that he come out. They showered his house with rotten fruit and eggs. Windows were shattered. Richardson appeared at an upstairs window with a musket. He threatened to "make a lane" through the crowd if they did not disperse. They responded by hurling a brickbat through a window. A rock struck Richardson's wife. Richardson aimed his musket at the crowd. No one believed he would shoot. He fired point-blank into the crowd. The shot struck and mortally wounded eleven-year-old Christopher Seider (or Snider), the son of a poor German immigrant. A nineteen-year-old in the crowd was also hit.

*A mob throwing stones attacks Ebenezer Richardson as he tries to pull down
the signpost boycotting Theophilus Lillie's store.*

The shocked crowd—now reinforced with people summoned
by the tolling bell of the New Brick Church on Hanover Street—
stormed the house. Only the intervention of William Molineux, a
leader of the Sons of Liberty, saved Richardson from a lynching.
Richardson was dragged through the streets to the Boston jail to
await the next session of the superior court, scheduled for March 13.
He would be tried for murder, because at 9:00 P.M., eight hours after
the shooting, Christopher Seider died.

A Propaganda Opportunity

Sam Adams was quick to see propaganda possibilities in the situation. He staged a funeral for the eleven-year-old boy that was
"the largest perhaps ever known in America." As many as two
thousand people marched in the funeral procession, led by the
Sons of Liberty and preceded by several hundred schoolboys.
John Adams was so impressed that he wrote in his diary, "This

[shows] . . . that the Ardor of the People is not to be quelled by the Slaughter of one Child and the Wounding of another."

Boston had already been a town pulsing with resentment. The child's death and its emotional aftermath elevated the tension to almost unbearable levels. "Things cannot long remain in the state they are now in; they are hastening to a crisis," Andrew Eliot wrote. "What will be the event, God knows."

Chapter 2

The Bloody Massacre
on King Street

A WEEK BEFORE CHRISTOPHER SEIDER'S death, Boston papers had published accounts of battles between civilians and British soldiers in New York City. Soldiers had torn down that city's Liberty Pole, and the citizens had defiantly replaced it. During one such brawl, two civilians were killed, but the Sons of Liberty had inflicted enough damage to humiliate the British soldiers, also known as Redcoats.

These newspaper reports—followed by the emotional display at Seider's funeral—added fuel to the already explosive situation in Boston. Fights between soldiers and Boston's "mechaniks" and laborers multiplied in the week following the child's death. The likelihood of a showdown increased with each passing day.

Countdown to a Tragedy

Of the two British regiments remaining in Boston, the Twenty-ninth was considered the especially tough and hot-tempered group. Governor Hutchinson himself had described them as "such bad fellows that it seems impossible to restrain them from firing upon an insult or provocation."

On Friday, March 2, 1770, Patrick Walker—a soldier of the Twenty-ninth Regiment—walked past John Gray's ropewalk, where unskilled Boston workers braided rope. Gray also frequently hired British soldiers to work for him during their off-duty hours. Boston laborers resented this practice. One of these town

30

workers, William Green, saw Private Walker passing by and asked him if he needed a job. Walker said that he did.

"Then go and clean my little-house [outhouse]," Green told the soldier.

"Empty it yourself," Walker answered, taking a wild swing at Green. Green whistled for his coworkers, and Walker was forced to flee after being knocked down and disarmed.

The mortified soldier soon returned with a dozen comrades. A fistfight followed, but the rope workers drove the soldiers away. Soon more soldiers—among them Privates William Warren and Matthew Killroy—arrived armed with clubs. The workers fought back with the heavy wooden slats they used to twist rope. Again the soldiers were driven off. John Hill, an elderly justice of the peace, convinced the workers not to follow. And at the barracks, a corporal managed to control the soldiers and get them inside. The fighting was over for the day, but both sides vowed vengeance.

British soldiers armed with batons and Boston rope workers armed with boards fight in the streets of Boston.

The next day, Saturday, March 3, Private John Carroll of the Twenty-ninth and two other soldiers fought with a group of workers at another of Boston's ropewalks. Once again the rope workers prevailed, and this time one of the soldiers suffered a fractured skull. Other confrontations occurred throughout the day. Lieutenant Colonel Maurice Carr, commander of the Twenty-ninth, wrote a letter to Governor Hutchinson warning that a crisis may be imminent. That evening, a rumor spread among the soldiers of the Twenty-ninth that one of its sergeants had failed to answer roll call, and may have been murdered by the waterfront toughs.

On Sunday morning, when the sergeant had still not returned, Lieutenant Colonel Carr led an unauthorized search for him at the ropewalk. It is unclear why Carr did this, because he later admitted that the sergeant had been seen alive on Saturday night. But Carr—as his letter to Hutchinson showed—was aware of the potential for violence. So he may have been searching for a stockpile of weapons. In any case, the soldier turned up on Monday alive and well.

The Fifth of March

On Monday, March 5, Boston seemed to be holding its breath. The word on the street was that both the soldiers and the rope workers intended to finish their fight as a matter of honor. During the morning, Hutchinson met with his council to seek advice regarding Carr's apprehensive letter. The council concluded that nothing could be done, because only complete removal of the troops would prevent further confrontations.

In the afternoon, the soldiers posted a written handbill: "This is to Inform ye Rebellious People in Boston that ye Soldiers in ye 14th and 29th Regiments are determined to Joine together and defend themselves against all who shall Oppose them."

By evening, all of Boston was waiting for something to happen. A foot of snow covered the ground. Chunks of ice lay scattered about. Boston had no street lamps, but the night was clear and the glistening snow reflected the light from a first-quarter moon.

On King Street, in the center of Boston, stood the Town House, where the council and governor met. One block from the

Town House was the Custom House that held Boston's official records—and where that particular night, Private Hugh White stood guard in the sentry box nearby.

To the south of the Town House, across a narrow fork of King Street, was the Main Guard, headquarters of the British troops. Two soldiers occupied the guard boxes. On Brattle Street, about three hundred yards from King Street, near Dock Square, stood Murray's Barracks, which housed part of the Twenty-ninth regiment.

Trouble in the Streets

An unusual number of people were out of their houses on the night of March 5, 1770. Bands of civilians and soldiers roamed the streets, looking for one another—spoiling for a fight. Around 8:00 P.M. the first incident of the night occurred on King Street, where Private White stood guard near the Custom House.

Captain Lieutenant John Goldfinch of the Fourteenth was on his way to Murray's Barracks. He passed by Private White's post just as a group of young apprentices, fourteen to fifteen

The Custom House, where Private Hugh White was lured into an altercation with a group of apprentices.

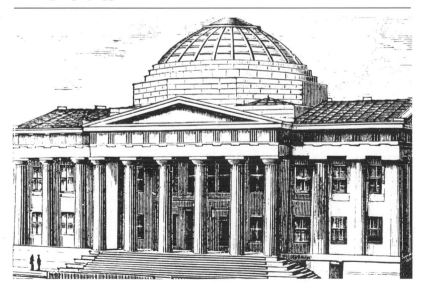

years old, arrived. One of the boys was Edward Garrick, a wig-maker's apprentice. Garrick shouted after Goldfinch, "There goes the fellow that won't pay my master for dressing his hair." Goldfinch ignored the taunt and continued walking. Garrick repeated the insult.

At this point, Private White took the bait and came to the defense of the officer. He shouted that Captain Goldfinch was a gentleman who paid his debts. Garrick gleefully responded that there were no gentlemen in the British army. White demanded that Garrick come closer and show his face. When the boy did, the sentry struck him across the head with the butt of his gun. Garrick staggered back from the blow, and then fled, sobbing, "I'm killed."

During this same interval, a skirmish occurred between sol-diers and civilians in Bolyston's Alley across from Murray's Bar-racks. Civilians hurled hard-packed snowballs at the soldiers, who defended themselves with shovels. An unidentified man raced back and forth past the barracks shouting, "Town born, turn out! Town born, turn out!" This was a rallying cry designed to summon Boston citizens. People flowed into the alley from all directions. Eight or ten more soldiers of the Twenty-ninth then rushed from Murray's Barracks to confront the crowd of people jammed into Bolyston's Alley.

Church bells began to ring all through the town. Bells ring-ing at night meant only one thing to Bostonians. Cries of "fire, fire, fire" immediately filled the air. People, who generally stayed inside, now poured out of their homes. Gradually, the word went around that there was no fire, "only a rumpus with the soldiers." Nevertheless, the shouts of "fire" continued. Some of the people returned to their homes, others remained on the streets.

By this time, Captain Goldfinch had reached Murray's Bar-racks. He was not a member of the Twenty-ninth Regiment. But being a senior officer and fearing a full-scale riot, he took com-mand and succeeded in getting the soldiers back into the bar-racks. The crowd lingered, taunting the soldiers with shouts of "You dare not come out." Soon, though, someone shouted, "To the main guard!" and the mass of people flowed toward King Street.

Meanwhile, about two hundred people congregated in Dock Square, the area between Murray's Barracks and Faneuil Hall. Some carried clubs. They gathered around a tall man wearing a red cloak and a white wig. (This man's identity was never established, though many suspected he was William Molineux, the radical leader of the Sons of Liberty.) After the man finished speaking, the throng shouted: "To the main guard!—that is the nest." They also sped toward King Street, where Private White, still under siege, was growing more frightened by the minute.

Private White Calls for Help

After the apprentice Edward Garrick had run away screaming, half a dozen boys had surrounded Private White, shouting, "Lousy rascal! Lobster son of a bitch!" Word of White's striking Garrick spread quickly, and the severity of the attack was exaggerated each time it was told. The angry crowd of boys increased to fifty or more. They pelted White with icy snowballs and shouted, "Kill him, kill him, knock him down. Fire, damn you, fire, you dare not fire."

Private White retreated from his sentry box to the Custom House steps, where he could see over the crowd and be protected from behind. He attached his bayonet and loaded his musket. The town watchman tried to reassure him by reminding him that the hecklers were only boys and would not hurt him. But White did not believe that. Pointing his musket and threatening to fire, he shouted for help: "Turn out Main Guard."

From the nearby Main Guard headquarters, Captain Thomas Preston, who was Officer of the Day, could see Private White's predicament. Preston was trying to decide what to do. One of his soldiers was in real danger, and he wanted to help him. On the other hand, Preston knew the hostile mood of the town. He feared that the sight of a squad of armed soldiers marching toward the Custom House would provoke a full-scale riot.

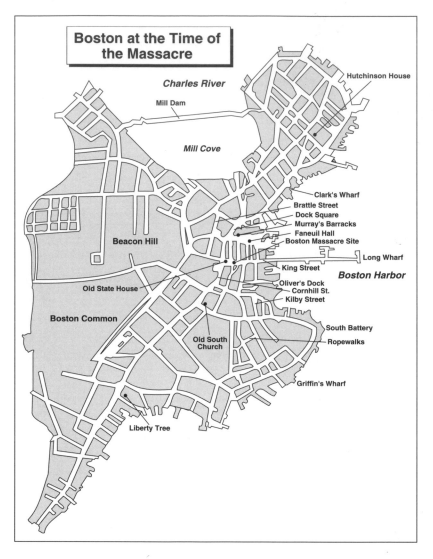

Boston at the Time of the Massacre

Charles River

Mill Dam

Mill Cove

Hutchinson House

Clark's Wharf
Brattle Street
Dock Square
Murray's Barracks
Faneuil Hall
Boston Massacre Site

Beacon Hill

Long Wharf

King Street

Boston Harbor

Old State House

Oliver's Dock
Cornhill St.
Kilby Street

Boston Common

South Battery
Ropewalks

Old South Church

Griffin's Wharf

Liberty Tree

As the screeching crowds from Dock Square and Murray's Barracks converged on King Street, Captain Preston made his decision. He ordered young Lieutenant James Basset to turn out the guard. After doing so, the inexperienced Basset asked nervously what his orders were. Preston first told him to "take six or seven of the men . . . to the assistance of Private White." But Basset was so obviously frightened that Preston took command of the squad himself.

The relief squad—all from the Twenty-ninth Regiment—consisted of Corporal William Wemms and Privates John Carroll, Matthew Killroy, William Warren, Hugh Montgomery, James Hartegan, and William McCauley. The squad moved forward with Corporal Wemms at the head so it would appear to the crowd that this was only a regular changing of the guard. They marched in two columns, with bayonets attached, but their muskets unloaded. Captain Preston marched beside them.

A Growing Crowd

The crowd that Captain Preston and his men approached was no longer made up of boys. Its number, moreover, had increased considerably. In later testimony, witnesses never agreed on the crowd's size. Jeremiah French, a captain of the Twenty-ninth who was on a roof overlooking the scene, estimated the crowd as being not "less than 300 or 400 people."

Among the crowd was Sam Gray, who had been involved in the fight at the ropewalk. Gray had come out in response to the church bells prepared to fight a fire. When he was told there was no fire but only "the soldiers fighting," he answered: "Damn it, I am glad of it. I will knock some of them on the head." Samuel Maverick, who was apprenticed to an ivory turner and was only seventeen years old, had also come out to help fight the supposed fire.

A number of sailors had joined the crowd, among them James Caldwell and one who called himself Michael Johnson. Caldwell, who had been visiting his girlfriend, was seventeen years old. Michael Johnson, whose real name was Crispus Attucks, was a large man in his late forties, sometimes described as black, sometimes as mulatto, sometimes as Indian. He had been in the thick of the action all evening. Earlier Attucks had led twenty or thirty sailors—some armed with clubs, as he was—up Cornhill Street to Murray's Barracks.

Some in the crowd tried to prevent serious trouble. Henry Knox, a young Boston bookseller and a radical, ran up to Preston. "For God's sake, take care of your men," Knox cried. "If they fire, they die."

"I am [aware] of it," Preston answered tensely.

Crispus Attucks was one of the men who died in the Boston Massacre. British troops shot Attucks after he hurled snowballs at them.

They Dare Not Fire

When the squad reached the sentry, the soldiers loaded their muskets. Captain Preston ordered Private White to fall in with the Main Guard squad. Preston then turned his men around and ordered them to return to the Main Guard headquarters. However, the crowd pressed so tightly around them that the soldiers could not get through. It was a dilemma. The soldiers could not withdraw, and the crowd refused to move.

Historian Page Smith re-created the scene in *A New Age Now Begins:*

> The noise, the shouting and clatter, the ringing of bells, the throbbing movement of the crowd as those in back pressed forward and those in front tried to prevent themselves from being pressed against the points of the soldiers' bayonets, the efforts of bolder spirits to gain a

place in the front ranks and of the more prudent to with-draw—all this presented a picture of hopeless confusion. [And] this took place with no more illumination than the moon and such . . . light as might be provided by torches and lamps.

In such an atmosphere the frustrations of the Boston towns-people, which had been simmering since the day the troops arrived, boiled over. "Damn you . . . fire!" someone in the crowd yelled. "You can't kill us all."

Battle at King Street

Captain Preston formed his soldiers into a semicircle. He stood to the side, slightly in front of the soldiers, and tried to reason with the crowd, tried to convince them to disperse and go home. The crowd answered him with curses and snowballs, and more taunts to go ahead and fire.

A Loyalist standing in back of the crowd supported the sol-diers. "Fire," he shouted, "I'll stand by you whilst I have a drop of blood."

But Sam Gray clapped a friend on the back and yelled, "Do not run, my lad. They dare not fire."

Most of the people in the crowd felt as Gray did. They were confident the soldiers would not fire without an order from a civilian magistrate. That was the law. They forgot, as Judge Trowbridge would point out in the trials, that "a man by becom-ing a soldier doth not thereby lose the right of self-defense."

Several in the crowd, seeking to avert tragedy, approached Preston. One asked if the soldiers were going to fire. Preston answered that they could not fire without his orders. Another asked the same question, and Preston repeated, "By no means, by no means."

At this point, someone in the crowd threw a heavy stick. It struck soldier Hugh Montgomery. He either slipped or was knocked off balance by the club and fell to the ground. Rising to his feet with his musket fully cocked, the furious Montgomery shouted, "Damn you, fire!" and pulled the trigger.

THE KING STREET SHOOTINGS FROM A PATRIOT VIEWPOINT

The radical Boston Gazette printed its version of the "massacre" on March 12. The following is an excerpt reprinted in *The American Revolution: 1763–1783*.

> On the evening of Monday, being the fifth . . . , several soldiers of the 29th Regiment were seen parading the streets with . . . drawn [swords] and bayonets, abusing and wounding numbers of the inhabitants.
>
> A few minutes after nine o'clock . . . Edward Archbald [and] William Merchant . . . were passing the narrow alley leading to Murray's barrack in which a soldier brandish[ed] a . . . sword of an uncommon size. . . . The soldier . . . struck Archbald on the arm, then pushed at Merchant and pierced . . . his clothes . . . and grazed the skin. Merchant then struck the soldier with a short stick . . . and the [soldier's companion] ran to the barrack and brought with him two soldiers, one armed with a pair of tongs, the other with a shovel. He with the tongs pursued Archbald . . . and laid him over the head with the tongs. The noise brought people together, and . . . more lads gathering, drove them back to the barrack. . . . In less than a minute ten or twelve . . . came out with drawn cutlasses [swords], clubs, and bayonets and set upon the unarmed boys. . . . One Samuel Atwood . . . asked [the soldiers] if they intended to murder people? They answered Yes, by G-d, root and branch! Thirty or forty persons, mostly lads . . . gathered in King Street. Capt. Preston with a party of men . . . came from the main guard. . . . The [people grew] clamorous and, it is said, threw snow balls. On this, the Captain commanded them to fire; and more snow balls coming, he again said, damn you, fire, be the consequence what it will! One soldier then fired, and . . . the soldiers continued [to] fire successively.

Montgomery's shot did not hit anyone, but the stunned crowd fell back. A frozen moment followed during which nothing occurred. Some said it lasted six seconds, others said two minutes. But most agreed that the interval had been long enough for Captain Preston to order the soldiers to cease fire. He did not. Moreover, Preston, who had been in front of the soldiers when Montgomery fired, had now somehow moved between or behind the soldiers.

The pause ended, and Matthew Killroy—one of the soldiers involved in the ropewalk affair—raised his gun and pointed it, apparently without aiming, toward Sam Gray. Gray's friend yelled, "Damn you, don't fire." But Killroy fired, and Sam Gray dropped to the ground with a hole in his head the size of a man's fist. Another shot followed immediately, and Crispus Attucks was struck twice in the chest. He crumbled to the ground, where he died with his head in the gutter that ran just in front of where the soldiers stood.

Someone in the crowd shouted, urging the civilians to charge before the soldiers could reload. As several started forward, more shots rang out. And James Caldwell, who was standing in the middle of King Street, took two musket balls to the chest. Patrick Carr, an Irish immigrant and an apprentice to a breeches maker, was retreating to a shop in Quaker Lane when he was struck by a musket ball that "went through his right hip & tore away part of the backbone & greatly injured the hip bone." Seventeen-year-old Samuel Maverick had started to run for home when a bullet

British soldiers fire upon unarmed Americans during the Boston Massacre. Two men died immediately and nine were wounded (three fatally) in the event.

A LOYALIST'S ACCOUNT OF MARCH FIFTH

Peter Oliver, whose brother Andrew had been forced to resign as stamp distributor five years earlier, was an avid Loyalist and a judge on the superior court at the time of the shootings. The following is excerpted from Oliver's *Origin & Progress of the American Rebellion, a Tory View.*

> According to common Custom, when a Riot was to be brought on, the [participants] would employ Boys and Negroes to assemble & make Bonfires in the Streets; & when all were ready, the Mob Whistle . . . would echo through the streets, to the Great Terror of the peaceable Inhabitants. Those Boys & Negroes assembled [on March 5] before the Custom House, & abused [the] Centinel; he called for Aid, & a Party of eight Soldiers were sent to him. This Party was headed by a young Officer; Capt. *Preston*, an amiable, solid Officer. . . .

> There were [400] or 500 of the Rioters collected; the Rioters pelted the Soldiers with Brickbats, Ice, Oystershells & broken Glass Bottles. Capt. *Preston* behaved with great Coolness & Prudence. The *Rioters* calling out *"Damn You fire, fire if you dare!"* & Capt. *Preston* [asking] them to be quiet, and ordering his Men *not to fire.* But at last, a Stout Fellow, of the Mob, knocked down one of the Soldiers . . . endeavoring to wrest his Gun from him, the Soldier cried, *"D---n you fire,"* pulled Trigger & killed his Man. The other Soldiers . . . supposing it was [the] Captain who gave the Order, discharged their Pieces, & five Persons were killed. [In] the trial great Stress was laid upon the Captain's giving the Order to fire, but there was no Proof of it. . . . Whether the Capt. Gave it or not . . . he [would] have been justified if he had given such Orders.

ricocheted and struck him in the chest. Two Bostonians were now dead; three were dying. Six more had been wounded, but would survive.

Gathering Up the Dead and Wounded

The Boston crowd could not take in what had happened. They could not believe that the soldiers had actually fired on them. Even the dead bodies lying before them could not penetrate their disbelief. One testified later that he thought the bodies were overcoats left behind by frightened people running away.

When people finally grasped what had occurred, some of them started forward, intent on picking up the dead and wounded. The soldiers, whether through habit or because they thought the crowd was going to charge them, reloaded and cocked their muskets. Captain Preston frantically ordered them to cease firing. He ran down the line pushing their guns toward the sky. He angrily demanded to know why they had fired without his order. The soldiers said they had heard the word "fire" and thought Preston had ordered them to shoot.

Captain Preston marched the squad of soldiers back to the Main Guard, and the dazed Boston citizens began to carry away their dead and injured. Boston had no hospitals. Patrick Carr, still breathing, was taken to a house in Fitch's Alley while someone else ran for a doctor. Samuel Maverick, coughing blood, was helped to his mother's boardinghouse, where he died a few hours later. Caldwell, the sailor, had no house in Boston. He would have been taken to a stranger's home to die.

Americans aid the dead and wounded as British soldiers look on in dismay.

Captain Preston, back at the Main Guard, could hear the town drums beating—calling out the militia and summoning the town's citizens to action. The crowd on King Street grew from a few hundred to more than a thousand as rumors spread that the British soldiers meant to massacre the whole town. The Sons of Liberty sent riders to outlying towns to ask for help. Preston called out the entire Twenty-ninth Regiment to face the ever-growing throng.

Governor Hutchinson Summoned

Many Boston citizens—both Loyalists and radicals—fearing more bloodshed, sought out Governor Hutchinson at his home. "Unless [he] went out immediately," they warned him, "the whole town would be in arms and the most bloody scene would follow that had ever been known in America."

Risking his own personal safety, Hutchinson made his way through the perilous Boston streets to King Street. At one point, he and those with him were forced to flee from a mob armed with clubs and cutlasses.

A frightening scene greeted the governor. The soldiers of the Twenty-ninth stood at the head of King Street, and a huge crowd of irate citizens filled the square. The people pressed around Hutchinson. He pushed his way through to Captain Preston. "How come you to fire without orders from a civil magistrate?" Hutchinson demanded angrily.

Preston answered, "I was obliged to save my sentry."

"Then you have murdered three or four men to save your sentry," one of the men with Hutchinson responded.

"The Law Shall Have Its Course"

Hutchinson proceeded to the Town House, where he addressed the people from the second-story balcony. He asked them to go home peaceably, promising that a full investigation would be carried out. "The law shall have its course," Hutchinson vowed. "I will live and die by the law."

Some listened. Others hissed, called him an enemy to his country, and refused to disperse. The people's initial disbelief

HUTCHINSON AT THE FRONT

The following is excerpted from Governor Hutchinson's report to British officials on the events of March 5. It is reprinted in James K. Hosmer's *The Life of Thomas Hutchinson*.

There has for a long time subsisted great animosity between the inhabitants of this town and the troops. . . . The 5th, in the evening near ten o'clock, one of the bells of the town near where I dwell was rung, and . . . in a few moments several of the inhabitants came running into my house intreating me immediately to come out or the town would be all in blood, the soldiers having killed a great number of the inhabitants, and the people in general being about to arm themselves. I went out without delay . . . to go to the Council Chamber . . . but [I] was soon surrounded by a great body of men, many of them armed with clubs, some with cutlasses, and all calling for their firearms. I [identified] myself . . . and endeavored to prevail on them to hear me, but was soon obliged for my own safety to go into a house and by a private-way into King Street. . . . After assuring [the people] that [an] inquiry should be made and justice done as far as it was in my power, and [convincing] the commanding officers of the troops in the street to retire with them to their barracks, the people dispersed. Expresses had gone out to the neighboring towns, and the inhabitants were called out of their beds, many of whom armed themselves, but were stopped from coming into town by advice that there was no further danger that night. A barrel of tar which was [carried] to the Beacon to set on fire was also sent back.

had worn off. Now they wanted revenge. The ever-present Son of Liberty, William Molineux, had also come to the Town House. He told Hutchinson that the people would go home only if the soldiers returned to their barracks. Hutchinson relayed Molineux's statement to Lieutenant Colonel Carr and added that he himself recommended this course of action. The troops were soon marched off, and, as promised, the crowd dispersed.

Captain Preston Jailed

Keeping his promise to the people, Hutchinson immediately summoned Justices of the Peace Richard Dana and John Tudor and requested the presence of Colonel Dalrymple, the commander of

British forces in Boston. Witnesses were called in and their testimonies taken. The sheriff was sent out with a warrant for Captain Preston, and at 2:00 A.M. Preston appeared before the
justices. Because some of the witnesses swore they heard Preston give the order to fire, the justices ordered the captain held
for trial. He was jailed at 3:00 A.M. The eight soldiers involved
had been confined to barracks and would be imprisoned the
next morning.

Boston's streets were finally quiet. But on King Street, the
frozen blood of her citizens—"near half a pail full in one
place"—cried out for vengeance.

Chapter 3

Uneasy Dawn
at Boston

AS DAWN CREPT OVER BOSTON on Tuesday morning, activities in the town differed from those of an ordinary weekday. Somewhere in Boston, Dr. Benjamin Church was performing autopsies on the dead, and Dr. David Jeffries was trying to save Patrick Carr's life. Sam Adams had taken command at Faneuil Hall, where thousands of the town's citizens gathered to demand that British troops

Faneuil Hall, where thousands of citizens gathered to demand that British troops be removed from their town.

be removed from the town. The stunned disbelief of the previous night had turned to rage, and a lynching mood hung in the air. Governor Hutchinson, recognizing that Boston teetered on the edge of outright rebellion, called a council meeting.

When Hutchinson reached the Town House, he was confronted by a delegation of Boston selectmen, or office holders, sent by Sam Adams to call for removal of the soldiers. The governor walked past them to his office, where the council waited. The council was divided. Some members supported withdrawal of the troops to Castle William; others wanted the troops kept in the town. Hutchinson told them he had no authority over the soldiers. Then, calling the town delegation in, he repeated that he could not order the soldiers removed.

Both Regiments or None

The selectmen delivered Hutchinson's answer to Sam Adams at Faneuil Hall, where the crowd had grown to three thousand. Adams decided to confront the governor himself. He selected the cream of Boston radicals to accompany him—John Hancock, Joseph Warren, and William Molineux.

When Adams entered the governor's office, Colonels Dalrymple and Carr were at Hutchinson's side, along with the twenty-eight council members. Adams delivered the town's message: "Nothing can . . . be expected to restore the peace of the town and prevent blood and carnage but the immediate removal of the troops."

When Hutchinson again declared that he had no authority over the troops, Adams reminded him that as governor, he was the commander in chief of all military forces in the colony. Colonel Dalrymple then offered a compromise. They would remove one regiment—the Twenty-ninth—since its soldiers had been the ones to fire upon the citizens. Adams responded: "If you have the power to remove one regiment, you have the power to remove both. Both regiments or none!"

Governor Hutchinson—who suspected that the so-called massacre had been arranged by the radicals for the sole purpose of driving out the troops—continued to stand firm. However,

Lieutenant Governor Thomas Hutchinson's reply to American citizens' request for the removal of British soldiers.

when the previously divided council unanimously agreed that the soldiers must be removed, Hutchinson had no choice but to yield. A jubilant Sam Adams carried the news to the townspeople, who then went "very Peaceably to their Habitations."

Within eight days all of the soldiers, except for those in the Boston jail, had been transported by barge and longboat to Castle William. Now the town's attention could turn to justice, which, to a majority of the people, meant convicting Captain Preston and the eight soldiers of murder.

Who Will Defend the Accused?

At the same time that Sam Adams was whipping the crowd into a frenzy at Faneuil Hall, his cousin John was visited in his law office by James Forrest. Forrest was a successful Loyalist merchant. He had come to ask John Adams to defend Captain Preston. No

THE TWO FACES OF CAPTAIN THOMAS PRESTON

Captain Thomas Preston was forty years old and had been a commissioned officer for fifteen years when he was arrested for murder. His commanding officer, Colonel Maurice Carr, described him as a "cool and distinct officer." But seven days after the killings, the endless lynching rumors panicked Preston. He wrote to the *Boston Gazette*, requesting them to print his message to the townspeople. It read, in part,

> Permit me thro' the channel of your paper, to return my thanks in the most public manner to the inhabitants . . . of this town— who throwing aside all prejudice, have with the utmost humanity and freedom stept forth [as] advocates for truth, in defense of my injured innocence, in this late unhappy affair that happened on Monday night last: and to assure them that I shall ever have the highest sense of the justice they have done me, which will be ever gratefully remembered.

Any Bostonians who believed Preston to be sincere in these remarks undoubtedly had second thoughts three months later. At that time the *Boston Gazette* and the *Boston Evening Post* printed a letter—obviously not meant for Boston eyes—that Preston had previously sent to England. Unlike his other letter, its contents, as the following excerpt reveals, indicated only contempt for Boston citizens.

> So bitter and inveterate are many of the Malcontents here that they are . . . using every Method to fish out Evidence to prove it was a concerted Scheme to murder the Inhabitants. Others are infusing the utmost Malice and Revenge into the Minds of the People who are to be my Jurors . . . [to bring about] . . . my Trial . . . while the People's Minds are all greatly inflamed, I . . . though perfectly innocent . . . having nothing . . . to expect but the Loss of Life . . . without the Interposition [intercession] of his Majesty's Royal Goodness.

lawyer in Boston wanted to take Preston's case. Loyalist lawyers feared being tarred and feathered by the Sons of Liberty, and patriot lawyers did not want to appear sympathetic to the Crown.

John Adams was a patriot, but he agreed to defend Preston and the soldiers. "I had no hesitation in answering . . . ," he wrote in his autobiography, "that Persons whose Lives were at Stake ought to have the Council they preferred." At the urgings of Sam Adams and other prominent Sons of Liberty, another patriot lawyer, Josiah Quincy Jr., also joined the defense team. That meant that Preston and the soldiers were represented by the best lawyers Boston had to offer.

But why would the radicals want "those men who had wantonly spilt the hearts Blood of *Citizens* like Water upon the Ground" to have the finest attorneys? Undoubtedly, one motive was to ensure that no one could charge the town with unfairness later. At the same time, the radicals believed they could trust fellow patriot lawyers not to examine the townspeople's actions on the night of the shootings too closely—as a Loyalist lawyer might do. Another likely reason was that they never considered the possibility of an acquittal. The radicals saw the slain men as martyrs, unlike the Loyalists, who saw them as five hoodlums who had been killed in a street brawl.

John Adams (above) and Josiah Quincy Jr. (left) agreed to defend the British soldiers.

The Loyalists evidently respected the reputations of John Adams and Josiah Quincy Jr. enough to trust them with Preston's defense. However, the venerable Robert Auchmuty, a Loyalist, would also be part of the defense team.

Depositions and Propaganda

The radicals had forced the withdrawal of troops from Boston and influenced the choice of counsel for the prisoners, but they did not stop there. Only days after the shootings, Paul Revere completed an engraving of the event based on a picture drawn by a young artist named Henry Pelham. A blood-splattered scene portrayed the soldiers grimly firing on a peaceful, cowering Boston crowd. Captain Preston, shown with his sword drawn, appeared to be ordering the soldiers to fire. The Custom House behind the soldiers was

Paul Revere's engraving depicts British soldiers aggressively firing on unarmed Americans during the Boston Massacre.

labeled "Butcher's Hall." The engraving was in great demand, and hundreds of copies were sold all over Boston.

The *Boston Gazette* added to the inflaming propaganda by printing a special black-bordered edition of the newspaper. The issue, illustrated with drawings of four coffins, proclaimed that "the streets of Boston have . . . been bathed with the BLOOD of innocent Americans."

Sam Adams, meanwhile, rounded up ninety-six eyewitnesses. One by one, the witnesses were brought before justices of the peace, questioned, and asked to sign written transcripts of their testimonies. Ninety-five of the ninety-six witnesses swore under oath that they had been on the streets that night for peaceful purposes only—visiting friends or attending church. And all swore they had

A *special edition of the* Boston Gazette *portrays four coffins surrounded by a black border.*

been attacked for no reason by armed British soldiers. Governor Hutchinson later complained that "no scrutiny was made into the [credibility], and characters of the [witnesses]."

On March 12, a town committee that included Sam Adams, Hancock, Molineux, and Warren wrote to Boston's former governor, Thomas Pownall. They accused the soldiers of being "instruments in executing a . . . plot to massacre the inhabitants." Then in a new twist, they charged that the customs officials had taken part in the "horrid massacre." "There are witnesses," the committee wrote, "who swear that when the soldiers fired, several muskets were [also] discharged from the [Custom] house."

Meanwhile, the Loyalists were not idle on the propaganda front. They had managed to sneak a customs agent aboard a ship to England. He carried a report from the military that contained its own depositions. It would be published in England as *A Fair Account of the Late Disturbances at Boston*. The "fair account" would put all the blame for the shootings on Boston citizens.

The Boston town committee hurriedly wrote its own twenty-two-page "official" report titled *A Short Narrative of the Horrid Massacre in Boston*. Printed in pamphlet form, with ninety-four of the ninety-six depositions appended, it was sent to England. The town then voted that all extra copies be impounded because if the report was published in Boston, it

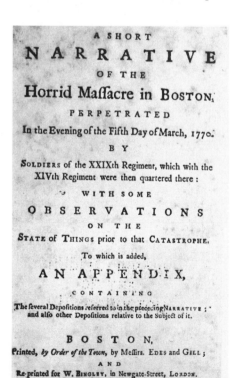

The title page of A Short Narrative of the Horrid Massacre in Boston. *Copies of the report were sent to England by the Boston town committee.*

might influence the minds of the prospective jury. The sincerity of the radicals is questionable because copies did ultimately circulate throughout Boston.

Criminal Indictments

The superior court began its scheduled session in Boston one week after the shootings. Chief prosecutor Jonathan Sewall presented indictments to the grand jury. These formal statements listed the criminal charges against Captain Preston and the eight soldiers, and also against four civilians accused of firing from the Custom House. The grand jury's task was to consider the evidence and then vote on whether the case merited a full trial or dismissal. The jury voted to indict all of the accused—Preston, the soldiers, and the civilians—for murder.

Who Will Prosecute the Accused?

After the indictments were handed down, chief prosecutor Sewall, either out of fear or because of his strong Loyalist sentiments, left town. In his place, the court appointed Samuel Quincy special prosecutor. Samuel Quincy, unlike his brother Josiah, was a Loyalist. The brothers also differed in their legal abilities. Samuel Quincy was not held in the same high esteem by the legal community as was his brother Josiah.

Alarmed at the possibility of inadequate prosecution of the soldiers by an inept Loyalist lawyer, Sam Adams and the patriots called a town meeting. The town voted to hire patriot lawyer Robert Treat Paine as a special attorney to aid "the King's Attorney . . . in the tryal of the Murtherers."

Patriot Hopes for an Early Trial Thwarted

The patriots wanted the trial to begin as soon after the indictments as possible. But Lieutenant Governor Hutchinson hoped to delay the trial until Boston's anger had cooled. In any event, the trial of Ebenezer Richardson, the customs informer accused of murdering a boy when he fired into a mob outside his house, was first on the court's schedule. Richardson had pleaded not guilty at his arraignment, and his trial had been set for March 23.

⚖ MASSACHUSETTS SUPERIOR COURT IN 1770

The Massachusetts Superior Court in 1770 was a circuit court composed of four judges. (Rather than a single judge, a "bench" of judges presided over trials.) As a circuit court, the judges held court in nearly every county in Massachusetts at least once a year. In larger counties like Suffolk (where Boston is located), the court sat more frequently. When the allotted time expired in one place, the court adjourned and moved to the next scheduled county.

In 1770, the sitting judges—all Loyalists—were Benjamin Lynde, John Cushing, Peter Oliver, and Edmund Trowbridge. Thomas Hutchinson was still the chief justice, but he had stopped participating in cases after being appointed acting governor.

Benjamin Lynde, age seventy, served as acting chief justice. He feared the mob. Twice he went to Hutchinson with his resignation; twice the governor convinced him "to hold his place a little longer." One year after the shootings, Hutchinson appointed him official chief justice. He served only one year before retiring and lived out his remaining days in the colonies.

Edmund Trowbridge, the most learned of the four judges, was considered New England's foremost expert on criminal and real estate law. He retired from the bench during the Revolutionary War and remained in the colonies without harassment.

Judge Peter Oliver, unlike the other judges, had never studied law. However, valuable political connections—his son married Hutchinson's daughter—had resulted in his appointment to the superior court. When Chief Justice Lynde retired, Hutchinson appointed Oliver the new chief justice. (One year later, John Adams would call for his impeachment.) Oliver "became extremely obnoxious to the people" and was forced to flee to England in 1776.

John Cushing, at age seventy-five, was the oldest of the judges. When he resigned from his judgeship a year after the soldiers' trial, he had served twenty-four years on the bench. Cushing remained in the colonies until his death at age eighty-two.

If possible, Boston's animosity toward Ebenezer Richardson surpassed its hatred of the soldiers. Consequently, no lawyer would defend him. Twice the trial was postponed. Finally, the court appointed a lawyer to defend Richardson, and the case was tried on April 6.

The jury found Richardson guilty of murder despite instructions from the judges that he could only be convicted of manslaughter.

Captain Preston and the soldiers, sweltering in the cramped Boston jail, could not have taken much comfort from the Richardson verdict.

Loyalists Delay Trial

When the court reconvened on May 29, all of Boston expected the trial of the soldiers to begin. But only two of the four judges—Benjamin Lynde and John Cushing—were present in the courtroom. Judge Edmund Trowbridge was ill, and Judge Peter Oliver had fallen from his horse—purposely, the radicals said. Court was adjourned until May 31. But on that day, again only two judges attended. Trowbridge was still sick and, strangely enough, Oliver's horse had fallen as Oliver was riding to Boston from his home. The radicals pressured Hutchinson to appoint temporary judges, but he refused. Again court had to be adjourned.

The patriots grumbled that the delay was intentional. Andrew Eliot, the patriot minister, wrote:

> Perhaps it was best to delay the trial at the first. The minds of men were too much inflamed to have given [Preston] a common chance. But they are as calm now as they are like to be . . . and if judges have power to delay trials as long as they please, it certainly is in their power to say whether there shall be any trial at all.

But Hutchinson and the Loyalists had won. Hutchinson wrote General Gage:

> I have given constant attention to the case of Captain Preston and the Soldiers and by taking . . . advantage of a number of accidental occurrences have produced without any Tumult a continuance of the Trial to the next Term.

For the court now had to move to another county. The soldiers could not be tried before August 28, when, by law, the court would be required to sit again in Boston.

Rumors and Arraignments

Two disturbing rumors circulated around Boston throughout the long, hot summer. One was that the mob meant to storm the jail

RICHARDSON TRIAL

The court appointed Josiah Quincy Jr. to represent Ebenezer Richardson. Quincy based his defense on the grounds that "a man's home is his castle," and a mob should not have the power to make him flee from his own house. It was an able defense, but Robert Treat Paine argued for the prosecution that the mob had not been a mob at all but merely a group of schoolboys.

At the trial's conclusion, the judges instructed the jury that Richardson could be convicted of no more than manslaughter because he had acted in self-defense. Judge Peter Oliver then delivered a tirade against the entire town and the failure of civil magistrates to control the mobs. Richardson, he asserted, was not even guilty of manslaughter.

Oliver's statement provoked an angry outburst in the crowded courtroom. As the jury left the room to begin deliberations, several spectators called out, "Don't bring in manslaughter!" Others yelled, "Hang the dog! Hang him!"

When the jury brought in a verdict of guilty, the disconcerted judges did not know if the jury had been influenced by the angry crowd or by the evidence. Accepting the jury's verdict—which they considered unjust—would mean Richardson must be sentenced to hang. But if they ordered the jury to reconsider its verdict, the judges feared a riot. Finally, they accepted the verdict but played for time by adjourning the court without passing sentence. (Later, after spending two years in jail, Richardson was pardoned by the king.)

---

and lynch Preston and the soldiers. The other rumor, which turned out to be true, was that Hutchinson had received a letter from England stating that if Preston and his men were found guilty, they would be pardoned by the Crown. This rumor made Preston uneasy. He feared a jury would be more likely to convict him if it believed he would be pardoned anyway.

On September 7, six months after the killings, Captain Preston, the soldiers, and the four civilians were formally arraigned—brought into court and asked to respond to the charges against them. Each pleaded, "Not guilty." When asked how they would be tried, each responded, "By God and my country," meaning that they requested a trial by jury.

At that point, for reasons never explained, the court—which still had ten days before it must move to another county—

adjourned. The adjournment meant that Preston and the soldiers could not be tried until October 23, when the court convened again in Boston.

This sudden adjournment upset everyone. Hutchinson and the Loyalists were troubled because if Preston was found guilty and sentenced to hang, the slow ocean travel in winter might keep them from receiving a pardon in time to halt the execution. The radicals, on the other hand, saw the adjournment as justice delayed one more time. And some began to doubt if a trial would ever be held at all.

Chapter 4

Captain Preston
on Trial

A T SOME POINT, THE JUDGES decided to try Captain Preston and the eight soldiers separately. How they reached this consensus is unknown. The judges may have been influenced by Preston's status as an officer and a gentleman, because the decision benefited Preston more than it did the soldiers. Or perhaps they reasoned that even though both Preston and his men were charged with murder, the charges would have to be proved or disproved in different ways, and therefore required separate trials.

The difference was that Captain Preston had not actually killed anyone. However, if the prosecution proved that Preston had ordered the soldiers to fire, the jury would have to find him guilty of murder since the soldiers would have had no choice but to obey his orders. Regarding the soldiers, there was no question that they had killed five men, but the prosecution had to prove that a *specific* soldier had killed a *specific* individual.

The soldiers understood the advantage of being tried with their captain. Although they could not testify themselves, a joint trial would give them the opportunity to challenge and question any witnesses who testified that Preston never gave the order to fire. Consequently, three of the soldiers submitted a written petition to the court, asking that they be tried with Preston:

> May it please your Honours we poor Distressed Prisoners Beg that ye Would be so good as to lett us have our Trial at the same time with our Captain, for we did

[obey] our Captains Orders and if we don't Obay [his] Command we [would] have been Confine'd and shott for not doing it. We Humbly pray Your Honours that you would . . . grant us that favour for . . . it is very hard he [Preston] being a Gentelman should have more chance for to save his life then we poor men that is Oblidged to Obay his command.

But the soldiers' request for a combined trial was denied. Two separate trials would take place. (There would, in fact, be three trials, the third one being that of the civilians accused of firing from the Custom House.)

In both military trials, John Adams and Josiah Quincy Jr. would be the defending attorneys, first for Preston and then for the soldiers. This would not be allowed in today's courts because of the conflict of interest. The conflict was that if the defense proved that Preston did not give the order to fire, it would then have to turn around and prove the opposite when defending the soldiers. Neither lawyer indicated that this was a problem, but both must have been aware of it.

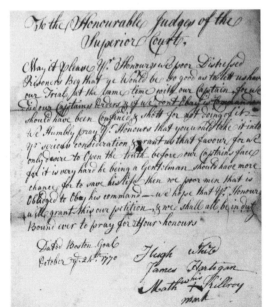

Three of the accused soldiers made a written request (shown here) to be tried along with their captain. Their request was denied.

Jury Impanelment

Captain Preston's trial began on Wednesday, October 24, 1770, at 8:00 A.M. The first order of business was to impanel a jury. A controversy arose immediately over whether the prosecution should be allowed to challenge jurors. No record of the court's decision survives. However, a look at the resulting jury indicates that the prosecution would surely have challenged certain jurors if it had been permitted to do so.

The court clerk ultimately drew twenty-four names for the jury panel. Two of these were rejected by mutual agreement. Out of the remaining twenty-two, the defense challenged fifteen. Only seven proposed jurors were accepted. Five seats remained to be filled, but the clerk had run out of names from which to draw. According to law, the sheriff then chose seven men from among the spectators. (Women were not allowed to serve on juries at the time.) Four of these men were challenged; the other three had acceptable excuses for not serving.

Packing the Jury

With five seats still vacant in the jury box, the sheriff and his deputies again sought potential jurors from the crowd. The outcome was that five Loyalists managed to get onto the jury. One of the five had even been heard to state that he "believed Captain Preston to be as innocent as the Child unborn," and that if he were on the jury, he "would never convict him if he sat to all eternity." The man was accepted despite this obvious bias.

The completed jury included six known Loyalists. (Five of the six would be exiled to England when independence was declared.) Only two Sons of Liberty sat on the jury. Why the radicals did not raise a ruckus over this jury packing and why Sam Adams was not even in the courtroom remain unexplained mysteries. Ultra-radical William Palfrey, who was in the courtroom, noted, "The management to pack the Jury was evident to every impartial spectator."

The prejudicial makeup of the jury seemed to leave little doubt as to the outcome of the trial. Nevertheless, Acting Governor Hutchinson expressed concern. He wrote to Governor Bernard in England: "I am afraid poor Preston has but little chance. Mr. Auch [Robert Auchmuty] tells me the evidence is very strong that the firing upon the Inhabitants was by his order."

Samuel Quincy Opens for the Prosecution

Unfortunately, no record of Captain Preston's trial has survived. However, Hutchinson ordered a summary of each witness's testimony prepared and sent to England immediately after the trial. Historians have used this summary, along with notes made throughout the trial by John Adams and Robert Treat Paine, to reconstruct what occurred.

According to courtroom tradition, Samuel Quincy—as the junior member of the prosecution team—would have given the opening statement. He would then have described the Crown's evidence, questioned the witnesses, and summarized the testimony, all before the defense presented its case. No record of Quincy's opening exists, but the testimony of the first witnesses indicates the prosecution's strategy.

Samuel Quincy was a junior member of the prosecution team.

Witnesses for the King

Edward Garrick, the apprentice who had been struck by Private White on the night of the shootings, was the first witness. He described what occurred and testified that he had seen soldiers in the streets carrying swords before Captain Preston called out the Main Guard.

The second witness, Thomas Marshall, a member of the Boston militia,

ATTORNEYS FOR THE PROSECUTION

Counsel for the prosecution were Samuel Quincy, elder brother of Josiah Quincy Jr., and Robert Treat Paine, hired by the town of Boston.

At one time, Samuel Quincy—like his father and younger brother—had been a Son of Liberty. However, he had long since been won over to the Loyalist side. He had been admitted to the bar on the same day as John Adams, but he never equaled Adams in ability. Samuel Quincy left the country during the revolution and went to Antigua, where he was appointed king's attorney.

Unlike Samuel Quincy, Robert Treat Paine was considered one of the outstanding legal experts of the day. At age thirty-nine, he had a thriving law practice in southern Massachusetts and was a legal rival of John Adams. Paine, who studied theology at Harvard, had served as chaplain to the New England soldiers during the French and Indian War. By 1770, he was quietly devoted to the patriot cause. He would ultimately sign the Declaration of Independence and later be elected governor of Massachusetts. Paine's prosecution of Preston and the soldiers did not reflect his superior abilities.

---

confirmed Garrick's testimony. He had seen two groups of soldiers that night—one on King Street and the other on Royal Exchange Lane—with "naked [unsheathed] swords." But it was Marshall's testimony about the actual shootings that was damaging to Preston's case.

> I heard one Gun. . . . A little space after [I heard] another, and then several. . . . Between the firing [of] the first and second Gun there was time enough for an Officer to step forward and to give the word Recover if he was so minded.

The prosecution apparently intended to prove that whether or not Preston had ordered the soldiers to shoot, he could have prevented the bloodshed. He had needed only to order the soldiers to cease firing during the interval between the first and second shot.

One of the prosecution's witnesses, Ebenezer Hinkley, proved to be more helpful to the defense than to the prosecution. Hinkley not only alluded to the rowdiness of the crowd, but more important, said that he "saw Preston between [the] people and [the] soldiers." The implication was that Preston would not have stood in front of the soldiers if he intended them to fire.

But Peter Cunningham, who followed Hinkley onto the stand, testified that he was "pretty positive" he heard Preston tell the soldiers to prime and load their weapons. Although Cunningham admitted on cross-examination that the officer giving the order had his back to him, his statement that the officer had carried no weapon and his description of the officer's uniform—red with a sash—served as an effective identification of Preston.

The last two witnesses of the day, William Wyat and John Cox, appeared to nail down the prosecution's case. Both swore without hesitation or qualification that they had heard Captain Preston order the soldiers to fire. Much depended on the witnesses' identification of Captain Preston. Throughout the trial, this identification seemed to hinge somewhat on whether or not Preston was wearing a neutral-colored surtout (overcoat). Wyat first stated that the captain was wearing such a coat, but retracted that on cross-examination. Cox stated unequivocally that Preston was not wearing a surtout but rather a "red Coat with a Rose on his shoulder." (Officers of the Twenty-ninth Regiment exhibited a single epaulet [ornament] on the right shoulder of their red coats.)

Sequestering the Jury

By the end of the day, only eight witnesses had been called (a substantial number by today's standards, but considered scanty in eighteenth-century courts). The realization that the trial would have to be adjourned until the next day caused a flurry of activity in the court. Not to finish a trial—even a criminal trial—in one day was unprecedented. Cases were always put into the hands of the jury by the end of one day. And under common law, jurors were to be deprived of "food, drink, light and fire" until they reached a verdict—even if it meant occasionally deliberating into the night, as had happened in the Richardson trial.

Because sequestering a jury had never before been necessary, hasty arrangements had to be made. The jury members must be isolated, but obviously they had to be fed and housed. Two keepers, one chosen by the prosecution and one by the

EIGHTEENTH-CENTURY COURTS

Certain practices of eighteenth-century courts seem unusual by today's standards. The person on trial, for example, was not permitted to testify, but *was* allowed to question witnesses. Unlike in today's courts, witnesses were allowed to remain in the courtroom while other witnesses testified. And witnesses were not necessarily called in sequence. For example, a prosecution witness might be called in the middle of the defense's case, or the other way around. If a lawyer wanted to call a rebuttal witness, he could do so immediately after a witness finished testifying for the other side. Cross-examination, too, was less prevalent than in modern courts.

Today when lawyers give their closing statements, they focus on the facts of a case. Any explanations of the law are left to the judges. But in 1770, lawyers were expected to expound on points of law and legal opinions. In some ways, judges had more power in the eighteenth century. They could order a new trial if they believed a verdict was contrary to the evidence.

Another common colonial custom was to use the courtroom as a political podium. Both judges and lawyers used trials to promote a specific political point of view.

defense, were locked up with the jury in the nearby house of the jail keeper. Bedding and food were supplied by the county.

Testimony Resumes

On Thursday, the second day of the trial, the prosecution's first three witnesses hindered rather than helped its cause. None of the three witnesses had heard Preston give the order to shoot, and all confirmed the unruliness of the crowd. But then the prosecution called its star witness, Daniel Calef. With calm certainty, Calef testified:

> I was present at the firing. I heard one of the Guns rattle. I turned about and looked and heard the officer who stood on the right in a line with the Soldiers give the word fire twice. I looked the Officer in the face when he gave the word and saw his mouth. He had on a red Coat, yellow Jacket and Silver laced hat, no trimming on his Coat. The Prisoner is the Officer I mean, I saw his face plain, the moon shone in it. . . . The officer had no Surtout on.

Calef had given a precise description of the attire worn by officers in Preston's regiment.

The prosecution next called Robert Goddard, who was considered by the town to be slow of intellect and lacking "ordinary Understanding." Nevertheless, his testimony was sure and unwavering. He swore that Preston stood behind his men with his sword drawn and yelled, "Damn your bloods, fire! Think I'll be treated in this manner?" Goddard held to his story during cross-examination, adding, "I was so near the officer when he gave the word fire that I could touch him. His face was towards me."

During the trial of the soldiers, Robert Goddard claimed that Captain Preston had ordered his soldiers to fire. Here, an artist's rendition of the event depicts the moment that led to Captain Preston's trial.

The prosecution had scored some direct hits with the testimony of Calef and Goddard, but then it floundered. The remainder of its witnesses had heard no order to fire. And one witness made matters worse when he insisted that Preston was wearing a surtout, thereby raising doubts again as to whether witnesses were confusing Captain Preston with someone else at the scene.

Prosecution Rests

The prosecution rested its case after calling fifteen witnesses. Samuel Quincy did not close with the usual summation of evidence. Instead, he quoted various legal authorities, including the renowned English jurist Sir William Blackstone: "Murder is . . . when a person of sound memory and discretion, unlawfully killeth any reasonable creature . . . with malice aforethought, either express or implied." In other words, even if an act is done without thinking, it can, in certain circumstances, be considered premeditated.

It was late in the afternoon when Quincy finished his summation. But instead of adjourning, the court directed the defense to present its case.

Witnesses for the Prisoner

John Adams opened for the defense. There is no record of his statement. Robert Treat Paine's notes indicate that it was also Adams who questioned the witnesses, but this is not known for certain. In any event, there was time to call only three witnesses before court adjourned for the day.

On Friday, the third day, the defense called twenty-two witnesses. None of the soldiers were called to testify, perhaps because they could have refused on grounds of self-incrimination, or more likely because the defense feared they would testify that Preston had ordered them to fire. Lacking any record, it is even harder to understand why the prosecution did not call the soldiers as witnesses. Or perhaps they did, and the court would not allow the soldiers to testify. Historians can only speculate about the possible reasons.

The defense called Joseph Edwards as its first witness. He swore that it had been Corporal Wemms who ordered the soldiers

ATTORNEYS FOR THE DEFENSE

Defending Captain Preston were John Adams, Josiah Quincy Jr., and Robert Auchmuty. Their credentials, especially those of Adams and Quincy, were unequaled in the colony.

John Adams was thirty-five years old when he accepted the unpopular task of defending Preston. In his autobiography, Adams lamented that accusations of taking Preston's case because it offered large sums of money had followed him all his life. "Preston," he said, "sent me ten Guineas and [after] the Tryal of the soldiers . . . eight Guineas more, which were all the fees I ever received or [was] offered . . . for fourteen or fifteen days labour, in the most exhausting and fatiguing Causes I ever tried." John Adams thought that defending the soldiers would destroy his political career, but he went on to become the second president of the United States.

Josiah Quincy Jr., at age twenty-six, was the youngest lawyer involved in the trials. Politically he was a radical, as was his father, Josiah Sr., who expressed shock that his son would "become an advocate for those criminals who are charged with the murder of their fellow citizens."

But young Josiah Quincy's devotion to the law outweighed his fiery devotion to the radical cause. He reminded his father that "these criminals, charged with murder, are *not yet legally proved guilty*, and therefore . . . are entitled, by the laws of God and man, to all legal counsel and aid."

The aging Robert Auchmuty played the smallest part in Preston's defense. Despite being the senior counselor and the only Loyalist on the defense team, he left the preparation for the trial and the questioning of witnesses up to Adams and Quincy. No doubt this was a relief to Adams, who, four years earlier, had complained of Auchmuty's "voluble repetition" and "nauseous eloquence" in the courtroom.

---

to load their muskets, not Captain Preston. Edwards's testimony, like that of those who followed him, would ensure Preston's acquittal. As Zobel notes, "[The] testimony generally was so strong that even an honest jury would probably have acquitted [Preston]."

Richard Palmes, a Boston merchant and Son of Liberty, was by far the strongest witness for the defense. A reluctant witness, Palmes testified that he was standing beside Preston when the first shot was fired.

I had . . . my hand on the Captains shoulder. I dont know who gave the word [to] fire. I was looking at the Soldier who fired. . . . The Captain might have given the word and I not distinguish [understand] it. . . . When I heard the word fire the Captains back was to the Soldiers and [his] face to me."

Palmes then cleared up the mystery of who was wearing a surtout. "I had on a Cloath Colored Surtout," he said.

Although Palmes never explicitly stated that Captain Preston did not order the soldiers to fire, his testimony was important because it would raise a "reasonable doubt" in the minds of the jury. The jury must have speculated that Palmes, standing beside Preston, surely would have heard if the captain had, in fact, given the order.

A second key witness for the defense was Andrew, referred to as a "Negro servant." Andrew had no last name, and he was

---

A copy of a summons for appearance handed out to potential witnesses during the trial of Captain Preston.

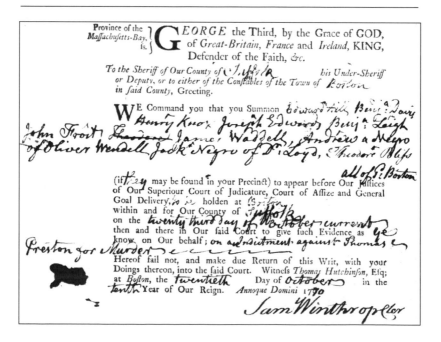

not a "servant," but a slave owned by Oliver Wendell. (Wendell's great-grandson, Oliver Wendell Holmes Jr., would one day be chief justice of the United States Supreme Court.) Andrew could read and write, and Wendell testified to his excellent character. Andrew gave a lengthy and articulate account that revealed the threatening mood of the crowd and the harassment of the soldiers. He admitted he could not see Preston's face when the word "fire" rang out. But he added, "I am certain the voice came from beyond [Preston]."

Captain James Gifford of the Fourteenth Regiment also testified on Preston's behalf. He said that if Preston had given the command to fire, the soldiers "would all have fired together, or most of them." Previous witnesses had testified that the men had their bayonets attached to their guns at the time the order to fire was given. Utilizing his right to question witnesses, Preston asked Gifford: "Did you ever know an Officer order Men to fire with their Bayonets [attached]?" Gifford answered, "No," which implied that Preston would not have given such an order.

John Adams Threatens to Quit

The defense team had to be pleased as the stream of witnesses continued to strengthen Preston's defense. And the radicals were undoubtedly relieved that testimony had revealed little about the behavior of Boston citizens on the evening of the shootings. But then, near the end of the day, several witnesses testified they had seen a number of townspeople on the streets that night carrying sticks and clubs. This testimony evidently took John Adams by surprise, and he angrily halted the questioning.

Josiah Quincy does not appear to have participated in questioning the witnesses. But he was the one who had prepared the witnesses to testify. Quincy argued with Adams over allowing such witnesses to continue, and Adams threatened to leave the case.

As a patriot, John Adams did not want certain activities of the Sons of Liberty exposed. He may also have feared such testimony would turn the jury against his client, or that it might

John Adams halted the questioning of his own defense team's witnesses because he was afraid they would reveal the Sons of Liberty's radical activities.

incite a mob to lynching. Moreover, Adams was certain he had sufficient evidence for acquittal without such testimony.

However, the behavior of Josiah Quincy, a patriot himself, is harder to understand. Perhaps he become caught up in winning the case. On the other hand, Quincy, like John Adams, opposed mob action. Despite his patriot beliefs, Quincy may have felt this was an opportunity to show the consequences of mob behavior. Whatever his motives, he yielded to Adams's demands, and the remaining testimony dealt only with what had happened on King Street itself. A short time later, the defense rested, and court adjourned for the day.

Closing Arguments for the Defense

When court assembled again on Saturday morning, October 27, John Adams gave the first closing argument for the defense. He reminded the jury that homicide was justified when a man was assaulted and could not retreat. He quoted Blackstone's principle that if in killing his attacker, a man inadvertently kills an innocent bystander, the law does not hold him accountable.

Adams also referred to testimony heard during the trial to strengthen his argument. If specific testimony had been harmful to his client, he merely pointed out that as witnesses people sometimes make honest mistakes. Adams made particular use of Richard Palmes's testimony, emphasizing that he was "an inhabitant of [Boston], therefore [he was] not prejudiced in favor of the soldiers."

Palmes's evidence had shown that Preston stood in front of the soldiers despite knowing that their guns were loaded. Surely if Preston had ordered the soldiers to fire, Adams argued, "self-preservation would have made [him] alter his place." He said Preston's failure to order the soldiers to cease firing after the first shot was due to "surprise."

The senior counsel, Robert Auchmuty, delivered the final summation for the defense, and the court adjourned for the Sunday Sabbath.

Robert Treat Paine, lawyer for the prosecution, gave the final summation in the trial.

Closing Arguments for the Prosecution

On Monday, the fifth day of the trial, Robert Treat Paine summed up the prosecution's case. Paine was ill, and his voice was almost inaudible in the courtroom. He noted that the evidence was complicated, and that both the defense and prosecution witnesses varied in their accounts. But he fumbled in his attempt to explain away the damning testimony of Richard Palmes, a Son of Liberty like himself. "Mr.

Palmes," Paine said, "is a gentleman who I can by no means suppose wou'd be guilty of a known Falshood, but he is certainly
mistaken."

Paine's most effective strategy was his effort to discredit
Adams's argument that Preston and the soldiers had acted in
self-defense to protect themselves from an abusive crowd. He
cleverly pointed out that Palmes had been standing in front of
the soldiers. "Wou'd he place himself before a party of Soldiers
and risque his Life at the Muzzels of their Guns," Paine asked,
"[if] he thought them under a Necessity of firing to defend their
Life? Tis absurd to suppose it."

Judges Instruct the Jury

Following the closing arguments, the four judges addressed the
jury. All of the judges spoke, but the main points were made by
Judge Trowbridge. He charged the jurors to consider several
questions: Did the soldiers constitute a lawful assembly? Were
the soldiers assaulted? Did the crowd constitute an unlawful
assembly? Did Preston order the soldiers to load their guns?

"If it remains only doubtful in your Minds whether he did
order the loading or not," Trowbridge said, "you can't charge
him with doing it." If Preston did order the loading, was it done
in self-defense? Finally, did Preston give the order to fire?

"If you are satisfyd that the sentinel was insulted and
assaulted," the judge continued, "and that Captain Preston and
his Party went to assist [him], it was doubtless excusable homicide, if not justifiable. Self-defense [is] a law of nature, what
every one of us have a right to."

All four judges agreed that the principal question was
whether or not Preston ordered the soldiers to fire. According to
Paine's notes, all of the judges told the jury it did not appear to
them that Preston gave the order.

Into the Hands of the Jury

Instructions to the jury had taken most of the afternoon, so it was
5:00 P.M. when the jurors received the case. Reportedly, the jury
reached a verdict within three hours, but it was not until court

reconvened at 8:00 A.M. the next morning that the jury reported its verdict: not guilty.

Considering the makeup of the jury, the verdict was not surprising. However, the evidence had also supported such a verdict. Even the ultra-radical William Palfrey, who had called the trial "nothing but a mere farce," admitted to having doubts. "In my own mind," he acknowledged, "there still remains a doubt whether Captain Preston gave the orders to fire."

Captain Preston was freed, but for his own personal safety and because of threats of personal injury lawsuits by relatives of the deceased, he sought refuge from both the litigation and the radicals at Castle William. From the safety of the fort, he wrote to General Gage: "I take the liberty of wishing you joy at the complete victory obtained over the knaves and foolish villains of Boston."

The townspeople grumbled about the verdict, but remained peaceful. This may have been because they did not feel as much animosity toward Preston as they did toward the soldiers. It was the soldiers the town blamed for harassing its citizens, not the officers. And the trial of the soldiers was yet to come.

Chapter 5

Trial of the British Soldiers

O N TUESDAY, NOVEMBER 27, 1770—three weeks after Captain Preston's acquittal—the soldiers' trial began. The courtroom on Queen Street, which accommodated approximately sixty people, was jammed to capacity. The lawyers for the defense and the prosecution were the same ones who had served in Preston's trial, except for one change. Sampson Salter Blowers had replaced Robert Auchmuty for the defense. Twelve new jurors were impaneled, and not one was from Boston. The clerk read the indictments to the jury, and the long-awaited trial was finally under way.

Case for the Prosecution

In Samuel Quincy's short opening statement for the prosecution, he reminded the jury that the soldiers were charged with "the wilful premeditated murder of five different persons . . . [and] they have [all] pleaded, *not guilty*. . . . It is my province [duty] . . . ," Quincy continued, "to give you evidence in support of this charge, and yours, gentlemen of the jury, to determine whether they are guilty or not."

Robert Treat Paine called the first witness. This opening day, the prosecution had time to call only six witnesses. Of the six, only Edward Langford, a town watchman, made a major contribution to the prosecution's case. He testified that he had been standing beside Sam Gray when Private Killroy's shot struck and killed Gray.

"Have you any doubt in your mind," Quincy asked, "that it was that gun of Killroy's that killed Gray?"

"No manner of doubt," Langford answered, "it must have been it, for there was no other gun discharged at that time."

When asked if Killroy had taken deliberate aim at Gray, Langford said no, adding that the bullet could just as well have hit him since he was standing right beside Gray. Langford also swore that Gray had not thrown anything at Killroy. "His hands were in his bosom, and immediately after Killroy's firing, he fell."

Francis Archibald, the last witness of the day, told about fighting with some soldiers on the night of the shootings. He denied seeing anyone in the crowd on King Street throw sticks or snowballs. At 5:00 P.M. the court adjourned.

Prosecution Continues

When court reconvened at 9:00 A.M. on Wednesday, James Brewer took the stand. He was a weak witness, unsure of his facts. The only thing he knew for certain was that the citizens had been yelling "fire," a fact that did more harm than good to the prosecution's

Written testimony taken from a witness the day after the Boston Massacre.

case. The prosecution was doing a poor job of following up on the town watchman's strong testimony of the previous day. To make matters worse, its next two witnesses contradicted each other.

James Bailey, a sailor, testified that Private Hugh Montgomery had fired the first shot "about where the mulatto [Crispus Attucks] fell." He said Montgomery had been struck with a stick and knocked down before he fired.

The next witness was Richard Palmes, whose testimony had aided Preston. He, too, testified that Montgomery fired the first shot, but he was positive that Montgomery had fired first and then fell.

It was important to the prosecution to show that Montgomery fired before he was knocked off balance, because the prosecution's case was built on the premise that the soldiers had fired without provocation. Quincy recalled James Bailey to the stand, but he stood firm in his statement that Montgomery had not fired until after he fell. The prosecution appeared to be faltering.

However, the tide unmistakably turned when Samuel Hemmingway, the sheriff's coachman, was sworn. He testified that a week before the shootings, he had heard Killroy say that "he never would miss an opportunity, when he had one, to fire on the Inhabitants, [and] that he had wanted to have an opportunity ever since he landed [in Boston]."

In its cross-examination, the defense tried to show that Killroy had not meant what he said. Hemmingway was asked if Killroy had been angry or under the influence of alcohol when he made those comments; Hemmingway answered that he was not. And he added, "I said he was a fool for talking so—he said he did not care."

Another prosecution witness, Nicholas Ferreter, testified about the brawl that occurred at the ropewalk two days before the shootings. In that encounter, Samuel Gray—the civilian allegedly shot by Killroy—had fought with Killroy. But describing Gray's conduct on the night of March 5, Ferreter said: "Samuel Gray, when I saw him that night was quite calm and had no stick."

Samuel Hemmingway may have been the witness who provided the prosecution with its most damaging evidence on Wednesday, but twelve-year-old John Appleton had to be the most heartrending. On the night of the shootings, Appleton said he and his brother had been sent on an errand to King Street. This is his description of what happened:

> Coming to Jenkins' Alley, my little brother with me, there came out about twenty soldiers with cutlasses [swords] in their hands, my brother fell and they run past him, and were going to kill me, I said, soldiers, spare my life, one of them said no, damn you, we will kill you all; he lifted his cutlass and struck at my head, but I dodged and got the blow on my shoulder.

Following the boy's testimony, court adjourned for the day.

Prosecution Completes Its Case

The prosecution resumed calling witnesses at 9:00 A.M. Thursday morning. It was the third day of the trial. The first witnesses swore they had seen Killroy the morning after the shootings (before the soldiers were jailed) and that his bayonet was covered with dried blood. The defense could have objected on the grounds that blood found on a bayonet twelve hours after an event does not prove that its owner is a killer. But no objection was noted.

The prosecution's final witness was John Hill, the justice of the peace who had tried to stop the fight at the ropewalk. He said the soldiers not only disregarded his orders, but "cut an old man who was going by." Asked if the prisoners had been among these soldiers, Hill answered, "I do not know that they were." On this somewhat weak note, the prosecution rested.

Concluding Arguments for the Prosecution

Samuel Quincy began his lengthy summation with a reminder to the jury that the prosecution had needed to prove that the defendants committed the acts noted in their indictments. In tedious detail, he then named each soldier and specified which witnesses identified that soldier. Then he reviewed the testimony of each witness.

Quincy made dramatic use of the testimony of young John Appleton. Calling Appleton the "little victim," the prosecutor used his evidence to show that

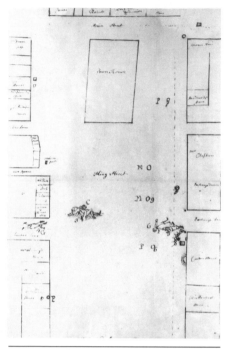

> the inhabitants had had reason to be apprehensive that they were in danger of their lives. . . . This apprehension together with the ringing of the bells, collected numbers of people . . . as is commonly the case when there is any [possibility] of fire. . . . This accounts for the number of people . . . and for some having sticks and canes. I mention this only to [refute] any evidence or pretence that may be made, that there was an intention of the people to assault . . . the soldiers.

Paul Revere's schematic drawing shows the placement of victims after the Boston Massacre.

Although there was no doubt that the soldiers had killed the five civilians, Samuel Quincy acknowledged that the prosecution had failed to prove which soldier killed which person—except in the case of Killroy, "against whom I think you have certain evidence." He added, however, that in the eyes of the law, all of the soldiers were answerable as accessories to murder.

Concluding his argument, Samuel Quincy told the jury that "on the evidence as it now stands, the facts . . . against the prisoners at the bar, are fully proved, and until something turns up to remove from your minds, the force of that evidence, you must pronounce them GUILTY."

In Defense of the Soldiers

As Samuel Quincy returned to his seat, his brother Josiah rose to present the opening argument for the defense. He urged the jury to remember that the very lives of the accused were at stake. He reminded them that anything that would justify a Boston citizen to fire on another citizen would also justify a soldier's firing. "And a soldier," he said, "need not have [an order from] a civil Magistrate any more than an Inhabitant."

Josiah Quincy sympathized with the jurors' resentment at having troops in Boston and with their anger against "certain measures . . . adopted by the *British* parliament." But he cautioned them not to let politics interfere with their purpose in court. "You are to determine [guilt or innocence] on the facts coming to your knowledge [in the courtroom]; You are to think, judge, and act, as *Jurymen*, and not as *Statesmen*."

After reviewing certain evidence presented by the prosecution, Josiah Quincy concluded his opening statement, and called the first witness.

Witnesses for the Defense

Before the day ended, Josiah Quincy called fifteen witnesses. Only two of these had actually witnessed the shootings on King Street. The remainder testified to the hostile and provocative actions committed against the soldiers throughout the town that night.

After court adjourned, Quincy, confident that the pendulum had begun to swing in favor of the soldiers, indicated his intention to continue the same line of questioning. John Adams, as he had done in Preston's trial, threatened to quit the case if Quincy "would go on with such witnesses who only served to set the Town in a bad light." Quincy agreed to confine his questioning to witnesses who had either been on King Street during the actual shooting or just prior to it.

Defense Calls More Witnesses

When court resumed on Friday morning, Josiah Quincy set out to establish that the soldiers had sincerely believed they were in danger from the crowd on King Street. One by one the witnesses were called, and one by one they testified in the manner of Nathaniel Russell, a chairmaker.

"Did the soldiers say any thing to the people?" Josiah Quincy asked Russell.

"They never opened their lips; they stood in a trembling manner, as if they expected nothing but death," Russell answered firmly.

Daniel Cornwall, a barber, testified that he saw the crowd throw oyster shells and snowballs at the sentry, and that just before the soldiers fired, he heard the people say, "Damn you fire, you bloody backs."

Newton Prince, a free black pastry cook, swore that he heard the people cry, "Fire, fire damn you fire, fire you lobsters, fire, you dare not fire."

The testimony continued in this fashion right up until court adjourned for the day.

Defense Completes Its Testimony

On Saturday morning, the defense continued to project the scene of an unruly crowd threatening the soldiers' lives. Then, around noon, Josiah Quincy called Dr. David Jeffries, his former Harvard classmate and a friend of both John and Sam Adams. Politically, Jeffries sympathized with the radicals, but he would be the star witness for the defense.

First, Quincy established that Dr. Jeffries had treated Patrick Carr during the ten days Carr survived after being shot by the soldiers. Quincy then asked what Carr had told Jeffries about the shootings on King Street. Jeffries answered:

> I asked him whether he thought the soldiers would have been hurt, if they had not fired? He said he really thought they would, for he heard many voices cry out, kill them. I asked him then . . . whether he thought they fired in self defence, or on purpose to destroy the people? He said, he really thought they did fire to defend themselves; [and] that he did not blame the man who-ever he was that shot him.

THE LAW AND DEATHBED DECLARATIONS

Massachusetts law permitted a witness to repeat a deathbed statement if it could be shown that the dying person had known death was imminent. That was the reason the defense asked Dr. Jeffries if Patrick Carr had been aware that he was dying. If Carr had not known, then Jeffries' testimony would have been ruled hearsay and disallowed.

Sam Adams later wrote: "It is to be observed, he [Carr] did not declare this under oath nor before a magistrate."

However, Hiller Zobel notes that Adams's allegation was irrelevant.

> Dying declarations are by definition unsworn; their admissibility depends not upon the sanction of the oath, but rather upon the premise, elegantly phrased by a later English judge, that no man "who is immediately going into the presence of his Maker, will do so with a lie on his lips."

Quincy asked if Carr had been aware he was dying, and Jeffries answered that "he was told of it." Then Quincy asked when the doctor's last conversation with Carr took place. Jeffries answered that it was in the afternoon preceding the night Carr died. He added that Carr "particularly said, he forgave the man whoever he was that shot him, [and] he was satisfied he [the shooter] had no malice, but fired to defend himself."

There is no record of how the spectators in the courtroom reacted to Jeffries' testimony. But it must have produced a stir, because a deathbed statement, then, as now, was not taken lightly.

After calling several witnesses of minor significance, the defense rested. And court adjourned until Monday morning.

Closing Arguments for the Defense

On Monday morning, December 3, the sixth day of the trial, Josiah Quincy presented the first closing argument for the defense. Quincy told the jurors he was aware that British soldiers had assailed and harassed Boston citizens in the streets on the night of March 5. He acknowledged that it would be human nature to want to punish the soldiers on trial for the actions of the other soldiers on that night. But that would not be acting according to the law, Quincy cautioned.

Quincy addressed the prosecution's charge that if one of the soldiers killed, then all eight were guilty. That only applied, he explained, when a group was unlawfully assembled. In a lawful gathering, Quincy said, "each individual of that assembly is answerable *only for his own act.*"

"It is . . . upon the right of self defence and self-preservation we rely for our acquital," Quincy told the jurors. He concluded with a quote from Shakespeare's *Merchant of Venice:* "The quality of mercy is not strained, but falleth as the gentle rain from heaven."

John Adams's Closing Argument

John Adams began the final argument for the defense by reminding the jurors of rules laid down by great English judges. "We are to look upon it as more beneficial, that many guilty persons should escape unpunished than [that] one innocent person

A depiction of the Boston Massacre again shows British soldiers firing with grim determination. The defense disagreed with this interpretation, arguing that the soldiers acted in self-defense.

should suffer," Adams admonished. "If you doubt of the prisoner's guilt, never declare him guilty; that is always the rule, especially in cases of life."

Adams quoted numerous legal authorities to explain the difference between homicide and manslaughter, to define lawful and unlawful assemblies, and to examine how far the law allowed one person to go in defense of another. He especially emphasized the right of self-defense, using Private Montgomery's situation as an example. "When he was attacked by the stout man with the stick [Crispus Attucks], who aimed it at his head, had he [Montgomery] not a right to kill the man?" Adams asked.

Adams had not completed his closing argument when, at 5:00 P.M., the court adjourned for the day.

Adams Continues

On Tuesday, December 4, the seventh day of the trial, John Adams proceeded with his closing statement. He turned from quoting law to examining the testimony of each witness in the case. He wanted to show that the soldiers had fired on the citizens because they feared for their lives. At the very least, he wanted to convince the jury that because of the soldiers' endangerment, they should be convicted of no more than manslaughter.

To the prosecution's assertion that "a person cannot justify killing, if he can by any means make his escape," Adams responded that the soldiers were surrounded by "twelve sailors with clubs" and had no means of escape. They were

> chained . . . by the order and command of their officer. . . . Clubs they had not, and they could not defend themselves with their bayonets against so many people; it was in the power of the sailors to kill [them] if they had been so disposed. . . . Would it have been . . . prudent [for the soldiers] . . . to have stood still, to see if the sailors would knock their brains out?

And what about Montgomery being the first soldier to fire? To make the jury understand what had confronted the young soldier, Adams dramatically depicted the scene:

JOHN ADAMS EXPLAINS THE LAW

In his closing argument, John Adams patiently led the jurors through explanations of the right of self-defense and the difference between homicide and manslaughter. The following is an excerpt.

The action now before you, is homicide; that is the killing of one man by another, the law calls it homicide, but it is not criminal in all cases for one man to slay another. . . . Felonious homicide is divided into two branches; the first is murder, which is killing with malice aforethought, the second is manslaughter, which is killing a man on a sudden provocation.

[It is] justifiable homicide; if . . . a sheriff execute[s] a man on the gallows . . . [because] it is his duty. So also . . . the law has planted fences and barriers around every individual. . . . That precept of our holy religion which commands us to love our neighbour as ourselves doth not command us to love our neighbour better than ourselves. . . . The rules of the common law therefore, which authorize a man to preserve his own life at the expence of another's are not contradicted by any divine or moral law. . . .

I have a right to stand [in] my own defence. . . . The law considers a man as capable of bearing any thing, and everything, but blows. I may . . . call [a man] a thief, robber . . . scoundrel . . . [or] bloody back . . . and if he kills me it will be murder . . . but if . . . I proceed to take him by the nose, or fillip [flick] him on the forehead, that is an assault, that is a blow; the law will not oblige a man to stand still and bear it; there is the distinction . . . as soon as you touch me, if I run you thro' the heart it is [only] Manslaughter . . . [because] it is an assault when ever a blow is struck, let it be ever so slight, and sometimes even without a blow.

When the multitude was shouting . . . and threatening life, the bells all ringing, the mob whistle screaming . . . the people from all quarters throwing every species of rubbish they could pick up in the street . . . *Montgomery* in particular, smote with a club and knocked down, and as soon as he could rise . . . another club struck his breast or shoulder, what could he do? Do you expect he should behave like a Stoick Philosopher. . . ? It is impossible you should find him guilty of murder.

Regarding the town watchman's testimony that Gray had no stick and stood with his arms folded when Private Killroy shot him, Adams shrugged that off. "This witness," he said, "is . . . most probably mistaken . . . and confounds [mixes up] one time with another, a mistake which has been made by many witnesses, in this case."

John Adams summed up his argument in these words:

> Facts are stubborn things; and whatever may be our wishes, [or] our inclinations . . . they cannot alter the state of facts and evidence: . . . if an assault was made to endanger their [the soldiers'] lives, the law is clear, they had a right to kill in their own defence; [even] if it was not so severe as to endanger their lives . . . if they were assaulted at all, struck and abused by blows of any sort . . . this was a provocation, for which the law reduces the offence of killing, down to manslaughter. . . . To your candour and justice I submit the prisoners and their cause.

Closing Argument for the Prosecution

It was noon when Adams finished and Robert Treat Paine, "much fatigued and unwell," rose to present the prosecution's closing argument. He told the jurors that he faced the most difficult task because "I am arguing against the Lives of eight of our fellow subjects." The defense, Paine said, was "well aware of their Advantage. . . . Observations . . . have been made in order to set the Prisoners in a *favorable* . . . light and bring them within the notice of your Compassion."

The defense had dwelt on the commotion in the town on the night of March 5, the large numbers of people, and the cries of "fire," Paine said. But he pointed out that it was the soldiers who first came out of their barracks armed with clubs, bayonets, and cutlasses and "in the most disorderly and outrageous manner were ravaging the Streets Assaulting every one they met."

"The King's Troops have . . . a right to march thro' the Streets and as such are a Lawful Assembly," Paine conceded. "But if in such marching, without just cause they fire on the

Inhabitants, and but one man is kill'd they Surely are all answerable tho it cant be proved who did the Execution."

Paine's summation was interrupted by the evening adjournment. But when court opened the next morning, Wednesday, December 5, he spoke for two more hours. He continued to challenge the defense's conclusions and then moved on to the possible verdict.

"The plea of Self Defence which is made for them [the soldiers] must fail unless you can be Satisfied there was no other possible way of Saving their Lives but by killing," Paine said.

The report of the coroner's inquest on the death of one of the victims, Samuel Maverick.

He told the jurors that if they believed Montgomery was knocked down before he fired as some had testified, then it was true they could find him guilty of nothing higher than manslaughter.

Paine then turned to the testimony against Killroy. "The Witness who testifys of Killroys killing [Gray] puts it beyond dispute that he shot him deliberately. . . . When you consider the evidence against *Killroy* . . . I think you must unavoidably find him Guilty of murder."

Robert Treat Paine finished his summation at 10:00 A.M. The jury was then subjected to three and a half hours of instructions from the four judges. The customary political comments took up much of that time, but those aside, the judges all agreed with Judge Peter Oliver's exhortation: "If upon the whole, ye are in any reasonable doubt of their guilt, ye must then . . . declare them innocent." At 1:30 P.M. the case was finally delivered to the jury.

Verdicts

The jury was out for only two and a half hours, returning to the courtroom at 4:00 P.M. The clerk asked if they were agreed on their verdict, and the jurors answered, "Yes."

"William Wemms, hold up your hand," the clerk said. Wemms did. The Clerk continued, "Gentlemen of the Jury, look upon the prisoner: How say you, is William Wemms guilty of all or either of the felonies or murders whereof he stands indicted, or not guilty?"

"Not guilty," the jury foreman answered.

One by one, the clerk called the names of the prisoners and received the same verdict: James Hartegan, "not guilty"; William McCauley, "not guilty"; Hugh White, "not guilty." But when the clerk reached Matthew Killroy, the foreman answered, "Not guilty of murder, but guilty of manslaughter." The roll call continued: William Warren, "not guilty"; John Carrol, "not guilty." The name of the remaining prisoner, Hugh Montgomery, was called, and the foreman answered, "Not guilty of murder, but guilty of manslaughter."

Matthew Killroy and Hugh Montgomery were returned to jail to await sentencing. The other six soldiers—some of whom undoubtedly had the blood of Boston citizens on their hands—walked out of the courtroom as free men. It had been nine months to the day since the "horrid massacre on King Street."

Chapter 6

Aftermath

BOSTON ACCEPTED THE OUTCOME of the soldiers' trial with unexpected calm. A handbill was posted during the night protesting the lack of justice and calling for citizens to "rise up . . . and free the people from Domestic Tyranny," but nothing came of it. And the day after the trial, patriots and Loyalists celebrated the queen's birthday side by side without incident.

Boston's placid acceptance can be attributed to several factors. The colonists now knew that Parliament had repealed the Townshend Acts. (Ironically, the repeal had been enacted on the day of the "massacre.") Moreover, the trial itself had convinced many—even some of the patriots—that the soldiers *had* been provoked into firing. And some people were simply frightened at how near they had come to an all-out revolution.

But without doubt, the main reason for Boston's tranquillity was that the troops no longer occupied the town. The tension that had risen to dangerous levels with the arrival of the soldiers disappeared with their departure. Only the Fourteenth Regiment, which had taken no part in the shootings, remained at Castle William. The hated Twenty-ninth had been transferred to New Jersey. And the day after the soldiers' trial ended, Captain Preston sailed for England.

Civilians Await Trial

But one loose end remained: the trial of the four civilians accused of firing on the crowd from the Custom House windows on the night of March 5. The defendants were Hammond

The Custom House tower is sandwiched between modern buildings in today's Boston. The town ultimately accepted the verdicts in the trial of the soldiers involved in the Boston Massacre.

Green, Thomas Greenwood, Edward Manwaring, and John Munroe—all Loyalist sympathizers.

The original allegation had implicated only Edward Manwaring and had stemmed from an accusation made by his servant, a fourteen-year-old French boy named Charles Bourgatte. Two weeks after the shootings, Bourgatte swore in an affidavit that three shots had been fired from the windows of the Custom House—two by himself and one by his master. He said he had been dragged up to the second floor of the Custom House by several men, and then forced by a tall man to fire two shots from two different guns out the window.

"He drawing a sword . . . told me, if I did not fire . . . he would run it through my guts. . . . After I fired the second gun, I saw my master in the room; he took a gun and pointed it out of the window; I heard the gun go off."

But when Edward Manwaring's friend John Munroe provided Manwaring an alibi, Bourgatte retracted his story. The boy was sent to jail. After spending one night in jail, he returned to his original story with the added information that Munroe had also been at the Custom House that night, as well as Hammond Green and Thomas Greenwood. Both Munroe and Manwaring provided alibis that showed they were not at the Custom House.

However, the Sons of Liberty had continued to press the case that shots had been fired from the Custom House. Consequently, Manwaring, Munroe, Greenwood, and Green were called before the grand jury. Despite the lack of any real evidence, the jury indicted the four men to stand trial for murder. They were jailed, but later released on bail to await trial.

The Third Trial

The third trial began on December 12, seven days after the soldiers' trial finished. Samuel Quincy conducted the case for the prosecution. From the records, it is not clear whether the defendants had an attorney. It appears they did not. Perhaps because of the flimsy nature of the case, they felt no need for one. The same panel of jurors who passed judgment on the soldiers served in the civilians' trial.

The prosecution called four witnesses. Samuel Drowne testified that he had seen "the flashes of two guns fired from the Custom house." However, Drowne's testimony was suspect because he was considered "dull-witted." Timothy White was called to establish that Drowne was capable of understanding. But White conceded that some people thought Drowne "foolish." A third witness, Gillam Bass, said he had seen the soldiers fire and he thought two or three gun flashes seemed "higher than the rest." However, he admitted that he saw no actual firing from the Custom House. The main witness for the prosecution was Charles Bourgatte, who repeated his previous statements. After his testimony, the prosecution rested.

At this point, the defendants requested the court to call certain witnesses in their behalf. Four men—including Edward Payne, who had been struck in the arm by a bullet that night—

swore they had been standing opposite the Custom House when the shootings took place, and they had not seen any shots fired from there.

Elizabeth Avery, who had been inside the Custom House that night, was called to testify. She denied that anyone fired from the Custom House. But more important, she swore that neither Manwaring nor Munroe nor Bourgatte had been in the Custom House on the night of March 5. To further substantiate this, Manwaring's landlady testified that both Manwaring and his servant, Bourgatte, had not left her house from the time the bells started ringing until after 10:00 P.M.

James Penny, an imprisoned debtor who had shared a cell with Bourgatte, clinched the case for the defendants. Penny testified that Bourgatte told him he had lied when he told the grand jury that Manwaring and Munroe fired from the Custom House. According to Penny, Bourgatte said he had sworn to the lie because William Molineux, a leader of the Sons of Liberty, had promised to free him from his master and provide for him. And Bourgatte also supposedly told Penny that Molineux had warned him that if he refused, the mob in Boston would kill him.

Charles Bourgatte denied ever talking to James Penny and asked the court to call William Page, a cabinetmaker who had also been in the jail. But Page did little to help substantiate Bourgatte's story. On the contrary, he confirmed that Molineux had taken Bourgatte into the jail keeper's house for a talk. Page did say Bourgatte told him later that "Mr. Molineux never urged or required him to say anything but the truth."

The evidence of both James Penny and William Page was hearsay, but no objections were made. This was probably because the contradictions in Bourgatte's story had completely discredited his testimony. Apparently there was not even a closing argument, and shortly before noon the jury "acquited all the prisoners without leaving their seats."

But Charles Bourgatte was jailed, and at the next session of the superior court, the grand jury indicted him for perjury. Bourgatte was sentenced to an hour in the stocks and twenty-five lashes at the whipping post. But the people did not want the boy punished. A Bostonian wrote in his diary: "This day the French boy . . . stood in the pillory [stocks]. [He] was to have been whipt but the Populous hindered the Sherif doing his duty." Nonetheless, two days later the full sentence of the law was carried out.

Killroy and Montgomery Sentenced

Privates Killroy and Montgomery had remained in jail throughout the civilians' trial. But on December 14, nine days after their trial ended, the two convicted soldiers were brought before the court for sentencing.

Manslaughter was a capital offense and punishable by death. The two soldiers were asked if they knew any reason why sentence of death should not be passed on them. They answered by pleading "benefit of clergy," a legal device that could be used by first-time offenders to avoid punishment.

This plea assured that Killroy and Montgomery would be freed after first being branded on their thumbs. The soldiers

BENEFIT OF CLERGY

Pleading "benefit of clergy," in which a defendant claimed to be a man of the cloth, originated as a protection for priests. It allowed accused clergymen to be tried in an ecclesiastical court rather than a secular court. When this led to abuses of the law, felons who pleaded benefit of clergy were no longer turned over to a church court, but were detained in prison until they received a pardon from the king. A later law allowed offenders using this plea to be released from prison after being branded on the thumb.

Defendants proved they were entitled to plead benefit of clergy by demonstrating they could read. When people other than the clergy began learning to read, the plea came to be used by anyone who could read—whether laymen and laywomen or clerics. Defendants proved their claim by reading a verse from the Bible, usually the first verse of the Fifty-first Psalm. This verse came to be known as the "neck verse," because reading it saved the defendant from hanging.

By the time the British soldiers were tried, benefit of clergy could be claimed in cases of manslaughter. The punishment called for the convicted offender to be burned on the hand and deprived of all goods and personal property. Because the plea could be used only once, the brand on the hand assured that the convicted felon could never again escape punishment by pleading benefit of clergy.

held out their right hands, and Sheriff Greenleaf burned the extended hands with a white-hot branding iron. John Adams, who was watching, said later that when the sheriff approached to do his duty, the young soldiers burst into tears.

Montgomery Solves a Mystery

With the last of the eight accused soldiers freed, Colonel Dalrymple wrote to General Gage that he would send them by sea to rejoin the Twenty-ninth Regiment in New Jersey. He was afraid to march them there by land, he told Gage, because "we have . . . too much reason to suspect their ententions to desert."

Although it did not come to light at the time, Private Montgomery did clear up one haunting question before he left Boston. He told one of his counsel that he was the man who gave the order to fire, not Captain Preston. Montgomery said that "being knocked down and rising again, in the agony from the blow he [had] said Damn you, fire and immediately he fired himself and the rest followed him."

Remembering an American Tragedy

Sam Adams and his followers had not gotten the verdicts they wanted, so Adams turned to the press. He published a series of articles in the *Boston Gazette* in which he criticized the way the court had conducted the trial, attacked the integrity of the witnesses, and bitterly expounded on the soldiers' harsh treatment of the townspeople.

And immediately after the soldiers' trial, Sam Adams began arranging for annual commemorative ceremonies to ensure that the horror of the night of March 5, 1770, would not be forgotten. For thirteen consecutive years, the "massacre" was remembered with elegant day-long orations as a reminder of the evil of standing armies.

As the years passed, the anniversary became a day of celebration, used to remind the people they must be diligent in protecting their rights and be willing to fight for them if necessary. For despite Boston's seemingly passive acceptance of the trial verdicts, neither Massachusetts nor the other twelve colonies

The grave of the victims of the Boston Massacre is located in the Old Granary burial ground in Boston.

forgot that the king's soldiers had spilled the blood of their fellow subjects.

John Adams may have overstated when he wrote that on the night of March 5, 1770, "the foundations of American independence was laid." Nevertheless, it cannot be disregarded that the memorial celebrations of the "Horrid Massacre in Boston" ended only when they were replaced with a more important celebration: Independence Day.

Epilogue

An Exactly
Right Verdict

THE BOSTON MASSACRE TRIALS represented a triumph of the law over mob violence. Beyond that, the fact that two reasonably fair trials could be conducted in the midst of such a politically hostile atmosphere gave credence to the colonial cause. Politics, even in obstreperous Boston, had been put aside, and the law of the land had been upheld.

Yet more than two hundred years later, historians continue to disagree over the verdicts. Were the verdicts just? Was a burn on the hand sufficient punishment for the deaths of five people? Can a trial be considered fair when the jury is packed in favor of the defendant? Is it a fair trial when the defendants are assured of a pardon even if they are convicted? Answers to these questions have been as varied as were the stories of those who witnessed the shootings.

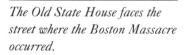
The Old State House faces the street where the Boston Massacre occurred.

John Adams had no such questions. In his mind, those guilty of murder were the British leaders who had sent troops to Boston. On the third anniversary of the Boston Massacre, he wrote in his diary:

> Judgment of death against those soldiers would have been as foul a stain upon this country as [were] the executions of the Quakers or witches [in the past]. As the evidence was, the verdict of the jury was exactly right. This, however, is no reason why the town should not call the action of that night a massacre; nor is it any argument in favor of the Governor or minister who caused them [the troops] to be sent here. But it is the strongest of proofs of the danger of standing armies.

Timeline

1765

March 22: England passes Stamp Act.

1766

March 17: Stamp Act repealed.

1767

November 5: Customs officials arrive in Boston.

November 20: First Townshend Act becomes law.

1768

June 10: John Hancock's sloop *Liberty* seized; customs officials mobbed.

October 1: British troops arrive in Boston.

1770

February 22: Ebenezer Richardson kills Christopher Seider.

March 2: Soldiers and Boston workers fight at the ropewalk.

March 3: Lieutenant Colonel Maurice Carr warns of imminent crisis.

March 5: Five civilians killed in the Boston Massacre.

March 6: Troops banished from Boston; John Adams agrees to represent Captain Preston and the soldiers.

March 12: A Short Narrative of the Horrid Massacre in Boston printed.

March 13: Captain Preston, the soldiers, and four civilians indicted for murder.

April 6: Richardson trial begins.

September 7: Captain Preston, the soldiers, and four civilians arraigned.

October 24: Captain Preston's trial begins.

November 27: Trial of the British soldiers begins.

December 12: Trial of the civilians begins.

December 14: Killroy and Montgomery sentenced.

1771

March 5: First ceremony commemorating the Boston Massacre held.

For Further Reading

Natalie S. Bober, *Abigail Adams: Witness to a Revolution.* New York: Atheneum Books for Young Readers, Simon & Schuster, 1994. An exquisite biography of Abigail Adams, "the wife of one president and the mother of another." Abigail Adams witnessed many of the events leading to the American Revolution. She and her husband, John, lived only a few blocks from King Street, the site of the Boston Massacre.

Alice Fleming, *Trials that Made Headlines.* New York: St. Martin's Press, 1974. Contains short descriptions of ten important trials in American history, beginning with the Boston Massacre trial and concluding with the Nuremburg trial.

Peter Charles Hoffer, *Law and People in Colonial America.* Baltimore: The Johns Hopkins University Press, 1992. A highly readable introduction to the origin of American law. Hoffer describes the growth of early American law from its beginnings in the British mainland colonies through the American Revolution.

Bonnie L. Lukes, *The American Revolution.* San Diego: Lucent Books, 1996. An overview of events that precipitated the revolution, the revolution itself, and the making of the Constitution.

Ann Rinaldi, *The Fifth of March: A Story of the Boston Massacre.* San Diego: Harcourt Brace, 1993. Fourteen-year-old Rachel Marsh was an indentured servant in the Boston household of John and Abigail Adams at the time of the Boston Massacre. In this exciting story, Rachel is caught up in the intrigues and dangers of those pre-revolution days in Boston.

Works Consulted

Charles Francis Adams, ed., *The Works of John Adams, Second President of the United States: With a Life of the Author*, vols. 2, 10. Boston: Little, Brown, 1850.

Bernard Bailyn, *The Ordeal of Thomas Hutchinson*. Cambridge, MA: The Belknap Press of Harvard University Press, 1974.

George Athan Billias, ed., *Law and Authority in Colonial America*. Barre, MA: Barre Publishers, 1965.

Catherine Drinker Bowen, *John Adams and the American Revolution*. 1949. Reprint, Boston: Little, Brown, 1950.

Richard D. Brown, *Massachusetts: A Bicentennial History*. New York: American Association for State and Local History, published and distributed by W. W. Norton, 1978.

Robert E. Brown, *Middle-Class Democracy and the Revolution in Massachusetts 1691–1780*. 1955. Reprint, New York: Russell and Russell, 1968.

L. H. Butterfield, ed., *Diary and Autobiography of John Adams*, vols. 2, 3, 4. Cambridge, MA: The Belknap Press of Harvard University Press, 1961.

Peleg W. Chandler, *American Criminal Trials*, vol. 1. 1841–1844. Reprint, Freeport, NY: Books for Libraries Press, 1970.

Harry Alonzo Cushing, ed., *The Writings of Samuel Adams*, vol. 2. 1770–1773. New York: G. P. Putnam's Sons, 1906.

Esther Forbes, *Paul Revere and the World He Lived In*. 1942. Reprint, New York: Book-of-the-Month Club, 1983.

Richard Frothingham, *Life and Times of Joseph Warren*. Boston: Little, Brown, 1865.

Harry Hansen, *The Boston Massacre, an Episode of Dissent and Violence*. New York: Hastings House, 1770.

Dirk Hoerder, *Crowd Action in Revolutionary Massachusetts, 1765–1780*. New York: Academic Press, 1977.

Peter Charles Hoffer, *Law and People in Colonial America*. Baltimore: The Johns Hopkins University Press, 1992.

James K. Hosmer, *The Life of Thomas Hutchinson, Royal Governor of the Province of Massachusetts Bay*. Boston: Houghton, Mifflin and Company, The Riverside Press, Cambridge, 1896.

Merrill Jensen, *The Founding of a Nation: A History of the American Revolution 1763–1776*. New York: Oxford University Press, 1968.

A. J. Langguth, *Patriots: The Men Who Started the American Revolution*. New York: Simon & Schuster, 1988.

Robert Middlekauff, *The Glorious Cause: The American Revolution, 1763–1789*. New York: Oxford University Press, 1982.

John C. Miller, *Sam Adams: Pioneer in Propaganda*. Stanford, CA: Stanford University Press, 1936.

Richard B. Morris, *The American Revolution: A Short History*. 1955. Reprint, New York: Krieger, 1979.

————, *The American Revolution 1736 to 1783: A Bicentennial Collection*. Columbia: University of South Carolina Press, 1970.

Edmund Quincy, *Life of Josiah Quincy*. Boston: Little, Brown, 1891.

A Short Narrative of the Horrid Massacre in Boston, Perpetrated in the Evening of the Fifth Day of March, 1770, by Soldiers of the 29th Regiment, Which with the 14th Regiment Were Then Quartered There; with Some Observations on the State of Things Prior to That Catastrophe. Originally printed by order of the town of Boston, 1770. Republished in 1849 with notes and illustrations by John Doggett Jr. Reprint, Freeport, NY: Books for Libraries Press, 1971.

Page Smith, *A New Age Now Begins*, vol. 1. New York: McGraw-Hill, 1976.

The Trials of the British Soldiers of the 29th Regiment of Foot, for the Murder of Crispus Attucks, Samuel Gray, Samuel Maverick, James Caldwell, and Patrick Carr, on Monday Evening, March 5, 1770, Before the Honorable Benjamin Lynde, John Cushing, Peter Oliver, and Edmund Trowbridge, Esquires, Justices of the Superior Court of Judicature, Court of Assize, and General Goal Delivery, Held at Boston, by Adjournment, November 27, 1770. 1807. Reprint, Miami: Mnemosyne Publishing, 1969.

Charles Warren, *A History of the American Bar*. 1911. Reprint, New York: Little, Brown, Howard Fertig Edition, 1966.

Kinvin Wroth and Hiller B. Zobel, eds., *Legal Papers of John Adams*, vol. 3. Cambridge, MA: The Belknap Press of Harvard University Press, 1965.

Hiller B. Zobel, *The Boston Massacre*. New York: W. W. Norton, 1970.

Index

Picture Credits

Cover Photo: Peter Newark's American Pictures

An American Sourcebook, Dover Publications, 11, 14, 15, 24

Archive Photos, 19, 33, 38, 73

Bequest of Miss Grace W. Treadwell, Courtesy, Museum of
Fine Arts, Boston, 63

Corbis-Bettmann, 17, 84

Library of Congress, 21, 22, 23, 27, 28, 43, 49, 51 (bottom, left),
53, 54, 61, 70, 77, 80, 88

North Wind Picture Archives, 15, 41, 91, 96, 97

Stock Montage, Inc., 31, 67

About the Author

Bonnie L. Lukes is a freelance writer living in southern California. In addition to this volume, she has written two other books published by Lucent Books, *The American Revolution* and *The Dred Scott Decision*. Her book *How to Be a Reasonably Thin Teenage Girl* was chosen by the National Council of Books for Children as an Outstanding Science Trade Book. She has also published essays and stories in a wide variety of magazines and newspapers. Her biography of nineteenth-century poet Henry Wadsworth Longfellow is scheduled for publication in 1998.

DISCARD